Undiminished Violence

The John Minturn Storm of 1846

By Thomas G. Clark

John Minturn/

John Minturn/

To Dick Stapleton, a fine sailor

Contents

The Wreck of the John Minturn

In the dark, foul winter of 'forty six,
Came full-moon, high tide at Squan Beach,
Three days of storm across the reach,
The north-east wind did wail,
And took ten tall ships or more,
The demon tempest hailed-
But the worst on Jersey shore, we learn,
Was the wreck of John Minturn,
A proud packet ship, dark bottle green
New York bound from New Orleans,
three masts and oaken keel,
Gruff Capt'n Stark behind the wheel,
With white sails like clouds in flight;
Through she cut salt-water like a sword,
Of the tragic fifty one on board,
Few lived to tell the tale;

How she struck the bar in dead of night,

And went down in the gale.

Now the clippers are long gone,

And their sailors sail no more,

On the sandy shore the old folk know,

How those fierce nor'easters blow,

And some still hear that awful sound,

The Minturn moaned, hard run aground,

Though they tried to get a lifeline through,

There was nothing for the surf-man could do,

But watch and wait, while the cruel wind blew-

And the proud ship, with her sails all torn,

Rocked widely in the raging storm,

The pounding waves like cannons roared,

All on deck washed overboard,

She broke apart and left her bones,

And Cap'n Stark met Davy Jones,

On that cold sand bar off Barnegat-

And there was nothing surfman could do,

But watch and wait, while the cruel wind blew.

Preface

Some time ago, I was completing some maritime research and I happened upon the following image. It depicted several shipwrecks that occurred off the New Jersey coast between 1778 and 1964:

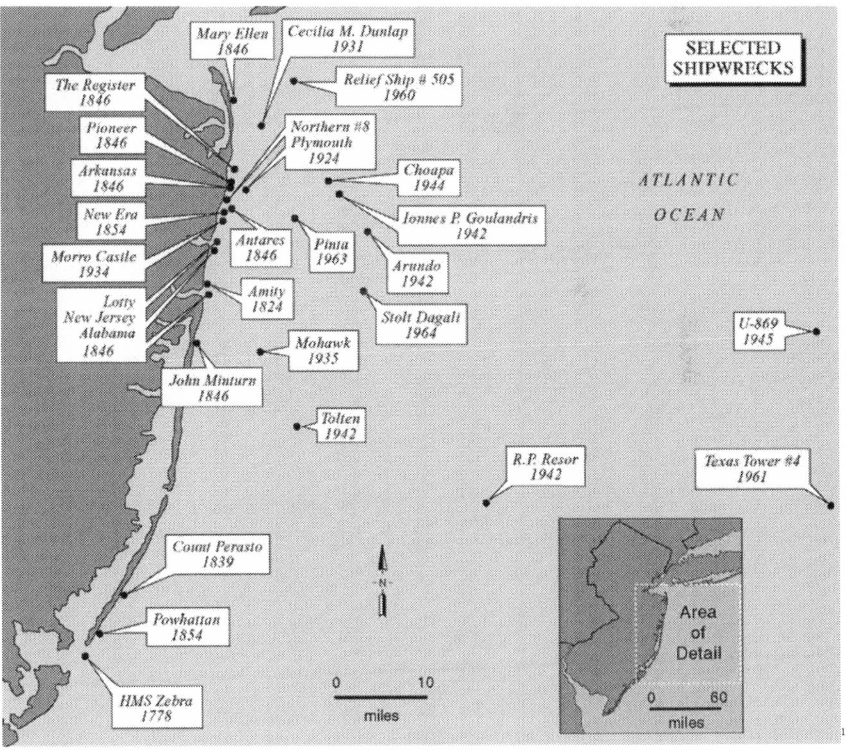

[1]

The map spoke to me because I grew up close to Sandy Hook. I witnessed several hurricanes and tropical storms and the damage they inflicted upon the shore, washing away tons of sand, damaging homes and compromising infrastructure. As a surfer, I ventured out to confront more modest waves and quickly developed an immense respect for their power.

But the ocean often wrote a conflicting narrative. On some days it could be as still as an alpine lake – not a hint of a wave, just the most subtle lapping of the tide upon the shoreline. Sometimes this calm would occur on the coldest of winter nights and fish would swim up to the shoreline within a net's reach.

A few days later the sea would boil with intensity, issuing mountainous, misshapen waves, which exploded upon the beach. For inland neighborhoods the air was infused with a salty mist that bled into your clothing and followed into the deepest portions of your lungs.

When storms like this appeared, we rushed to the boardwalk looking for the maritime drama that would play out before us – a ship doing battle with the storm. Sometimes we found a far-off vessel pitching awkwardly atop a wave crest, only to then drop out of sight. It would finally reappear after what seemed to be entire minutes. However from our perspective, it seemed to be stationary making no forward progress in its fight against wind, waves and tide.

We could only imagine the anxiety the crew was experiencing aboard these vessels; it was well beyond our beachcomber ken. We were denizens of the shore, our association with the ocean brief and recreational, protected by lifeguards and jetties, and in conditions of our own choosing.

But the crews aboard these ships had to respond to whatever conditions presented, and avoid adding their vessel's name to the map of New Jersey shipwrecks.

When I examined the details of the "Selected Shipwrecks"[2] map more closely, I recognized the name of only one ship, the *Morro Castle*. This 1934 disaster merited national headlines at the time, largely because the tragedy played out over many days near popular seaside communities.

GOOD EVENING

THE STAR JOURNAL

200 DEAD IN LINER FIRE

PASSENGERS ON MORRO CASTLE TRAPPED

SURVIVORS ON RESCUE SHIPS OR LANDED ON NEW JERSEY COAST

The Weather

FINISH FIGHT IN TEXTILE STRIKE SEEN

FIRE DESTROYS PALATIAL LINER

LIGHTNING STRUCK SHIP CARRYING 576 PERSONS, HAVANA TO NEW YORK

The *Morro Castle* disaster claimed 137 lives (not 200 as reported in some newspapers). Several unrelated factors contributed to the tragedy: the unexpected death the night before of the ship's captain, an approaching nor'easter, and, most critically, a small fire in a storage locker that would quickly engulf the entire ship (not lightning, as was reported in several newspapers). The remains of the burned hull washed ashore in Asbury Park, and the image was seared into the memories of everyone who were there. Along with the famous photograph of the *Hindenburg*, this image is probably the most recognized depiction of a New Jersey disaster.

As I looked more closely at the other listed shipwrecks, two distinct patterns emerged. The first was a cluster of wrecks that occurred in the 1940's: three in 1942 and one in 1944. Some quick research revealed these were the result of German U-Boat activity.

For instance, one of the wrecks was the *R.P. Resor;* an oil freighter tricked by the Germans into thinking it was a local fishing boat. This enabled the U-boat to move closer and discharge several torpedoes, resulting in the loss of forty-eight sailors.

Four of the wrecks from that period shared one commonality; their demise was man-made, either intentionally or attributed as accidental. They only differed by their location and the time of their demise.

But the next large grouping was significantly different. Suddenly they jumped off the page, as if to self-select. Notably, nine of the twenty-four shipwrecks appeared to cluster on the shoreline, and oddly, they were all lost in the same year; 1846. Further research revealed that the wrecks occurred on February 15th. I wondered what event had caused more than one-third of the most significant wrecks in New Jersey history to appear on the map.

The 1846 event would later be referred to as the "Minturn Storm", after the ship *John Minturn*, which was completing its February run from New Orleans to New York. The storm would claim upwards of sixty lives, but its reach was just as noteworthy; the effects were felt along the coast from the Carolinas to Massachusetts, and inland from Richmond, Virginia to Syracuse, New York.

The storm was a classic winter nor'easter, originating off the southern U.S. coast, gaining strength as it barreled northward. It brought bone-chilling temperatures, blizzard conditions and significant snowfall that blanketed villages, towns and cities.

But its effects were greatest at sea. Nine vessels would be lost along the New Jersey coast alone. Other ships also fell victim to the storm, although the greatest loss of life occurred in this narrow twenty-mile swath.

Undiminished Violence details the events that led up to the storm, the demise of the ships and the individuals who were lost on that fateful February day. But it goes beyond mere descriptions of the meteorological and nautical conditions. The book attempts to provide some modest context of the social, scientific and technological events of the day. In addition, it reports on the political ramifications of the disaster, both at the local and national level.

In the final chapters and epilogue, *Undiminished Violence* seeks to complete the unfinished narrative of the major actors in the *Minturn* saga. Some of the victims had cheated death just weeks before, while financial pressures and political prejudices contributed to the demise of the *John Minturn* itself.

The book's purpose is to stitch together all the disparate facts surrounding the great storm and the loss of the New Jersey ships. By bringing together the realities surrounding the ships, the crews, the heroes and the questionable judgments, only then can one truly understand what occurred on that horrific Sunday, February 15, 1846.

The Beginnings of Bad Luck

Joseph P. Babcock was born in 1812, the year the fledging United States declared war against mighty Great Britain. Babcock hailed from the modest Rhode Island town of North Kingston, situated to the west of Newport and to the south of Providence, the two newly founded cities linked by the waters of the sprawling Narragansett Bay.

As a young boy, Joseph climbed one of the nearby observation points – Mount View – and watched the schooners, brigs, barks and whalers dart across the bay. Their number, variety and constant motion instilled in Joseph a great curiosity. Where had they come from? What treasures did they carry? And why were they visiting his little corner of the world? The experience also led Joseph to wonder what lay beyond the bay's placid waters.

Although Joseph could not articulate it at the time, the Atlantic Ocean was beckoning him to explore further. He understood the ocean provided a pathway not just to the great cities of Boston and New York, but also to more exotic destinations of South America, Europe and even far-off Asia. His interest eventually matured into a definitive plan to command a ship of his own one day.

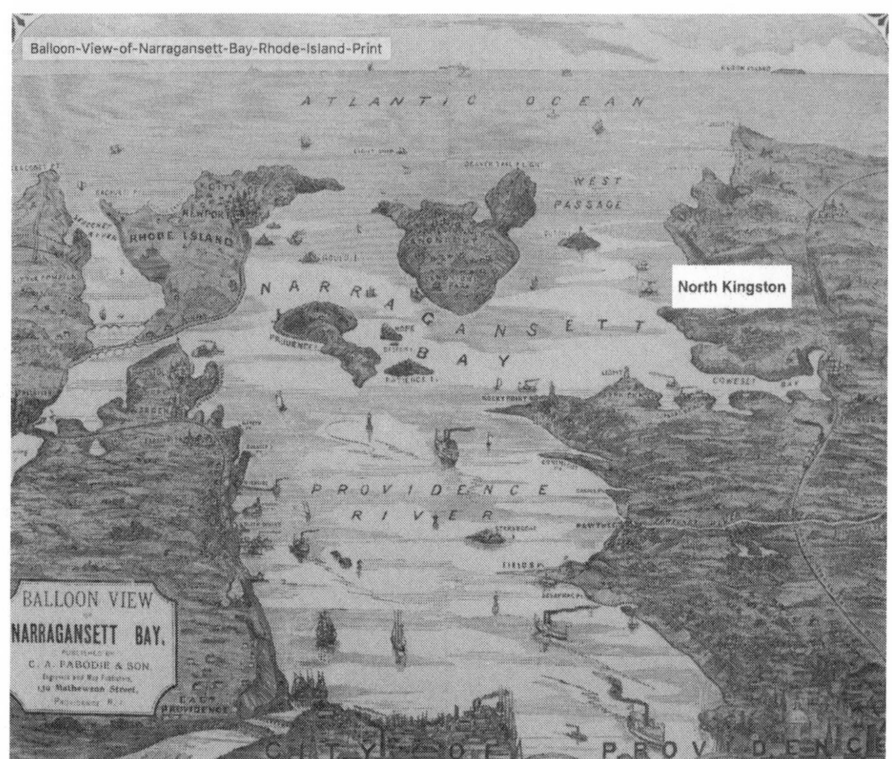

A view of Narragansett Bay, looking south. Providence is on bottom right of the image, Newport on the upper left.

Many years later that day arrived. Babcock left the confinement of the bay for New York City, where he assumed command of the schooner *Van Buren*. In 1843, he proudly sailed the *Van Buren* down the east coast, stopping briefly in Key West, Florida. From there he turned the vessel due west and entered the warm and tamer waters of the Gulf of Mexico. Here he would spend the next two years shuttling from his base in New Orleans to various ports along the southern portion of the U.S.

In the Gulf, he left behind the brutal New England winters he remembered as a child; those fierce nor'easters that gouged the shoreline and swallowed vessels whole. When the nor'easters weren't present, persistent icing made a ship's decks treacherous to traverse, and fouled the ship's blocks and stays.

However, he understood the Gulf also had hurricanes that raged in late summer, but they usually came with advance warning. Since he generally hugged the coastline, he could retreat to a nearby port if a storm arose.

Joseph had somehow managed to trade the frigid hazards of the north for the warm temperatures and mild seas of the south. The bargain was clearly in his favor and he was grateful for his good fortune.

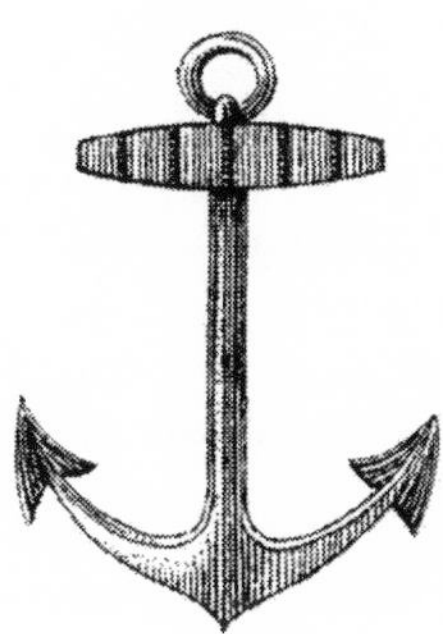

He was also grateful the ship's owner had provided him with a generous amount of work. Together they transacted business with merchants in the ports of Pensacola, New Orleans, Galveston and Corpus Christie.

But it was a particular trip to Corpus Christie that would change the course of Joseph's life.

All was going well for the *Van Buren*, until the ship and Joseph's name appeared in the October 1845 "Disaster column" of several newspapers. Ironically, the column was often the first read by avaricious merchants and anxious family members. This particular one read as follows:

ct on cargo recovered by diving.

Sch Van Buren, Babcock, for New Orleans, was capsized and totally lost in going out over Aransas Bar, in tow of steam sch Augusta; passengers and crew saved and landed on St Joseph's island. Several vessels lying off Aransas Bar had been compelled to slip their cables prev to 1st inst, and put to sea, most of which suffered more or less damage before they could get back to their anchorage.

[3]

Transcripton:

Sch Van Buren, Babcock, for New Orleans, was capsized and totally lost in going out over Aransas Bar, in tow of steam sch Augusta; passengers and crew saved and landed on St. Joseph's island. Several vessels lying off Aransas Bar had been compelled to slip their cables prev to 1st inst, and put to sea, most of which suffered more or less damage before they could get back to their anchorage.

On a return trip to New Orleans, the *Van Buren* had capsized. At the time, she was in tow behind the steamship, *Augusta,* as they attempted to cross the Aransas Bar, a shoal near present-day Corpus Christie.

Fortunately, there was no loss of life and those aboard were temporarily transferred to the remote island of St. Joseph's (present day St. Jose). From there they were eventually delivered to other vessels and ports.

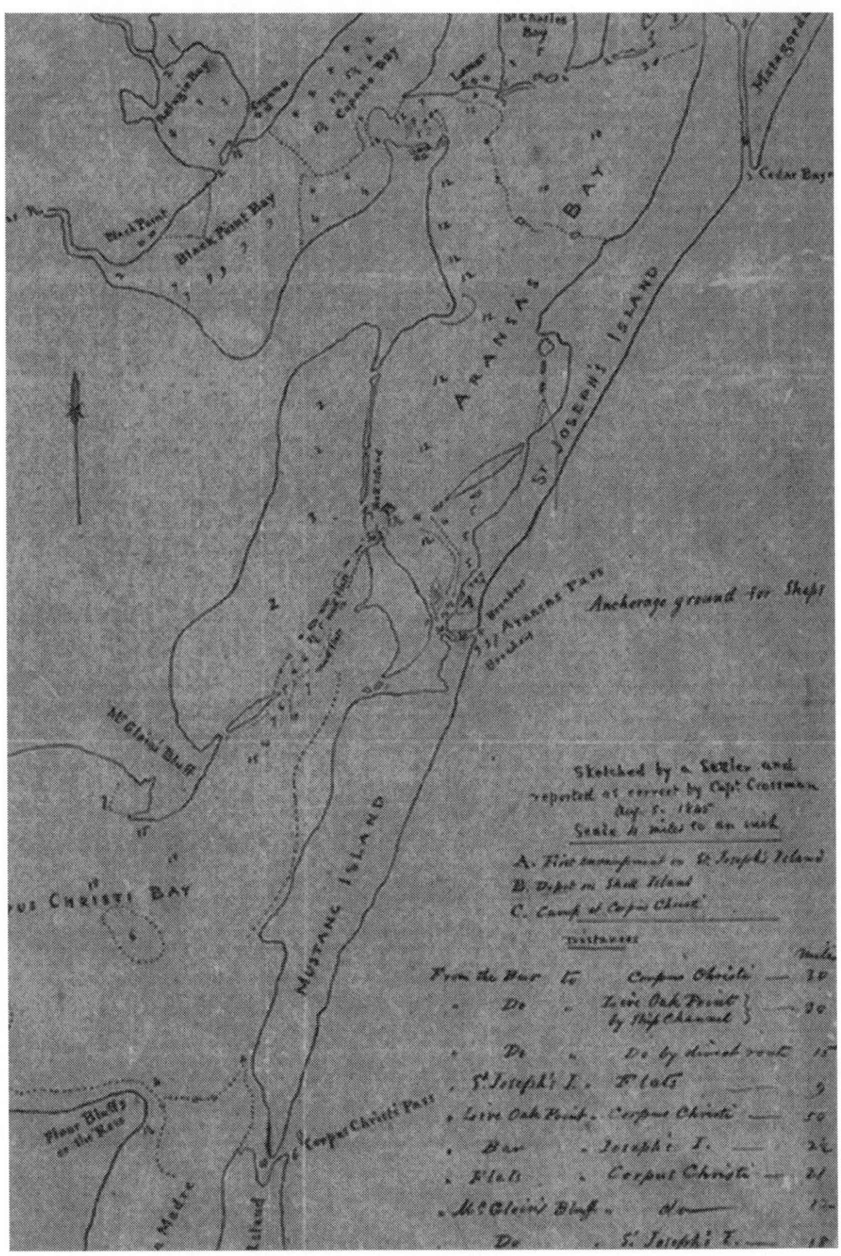

Period map of St. Joseph's Island, near Corpus Christie

Babcock and first mate Nicholas Frye Baker returned to New Orleans, where they sought northbound passage to New York. Their purpose was twofold: to explain to the *Van Buren's* owners the mishap, and to secure future employment.

On the New Orleans docks, the two men learned of the *John Minturn's* voyage to New York in a few weeks' time, and they purchased passage. Little did they know that this trip would also prove to be disastrous – and far, far worse than their last experience on the *Van Buren.*

Ominously, in just a few short weeks, the *John Minturn* would itself be listed in the disaster column of newspapers far and wide.

The 415-ton ship, *Cherokee,* was built in Medford, Massachusetts, and proudly owned by the successful shipping merchant, Bramhall & Howe, along with several others.

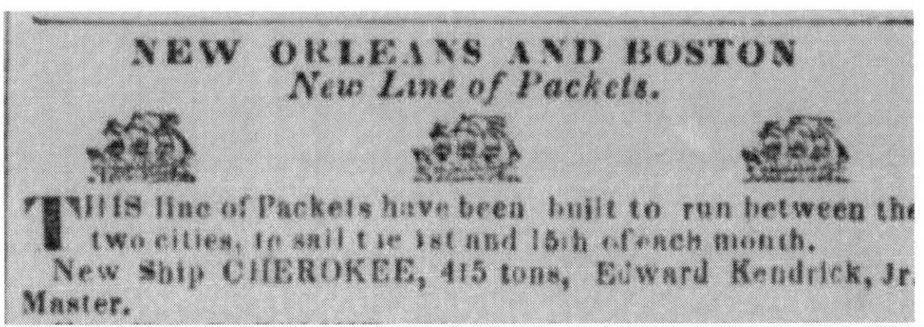

NEW ORLEANS AND BOSTON
New Line of Packets.

THIS line of Packets have been built to run between the two cities, to sail the 1st and 15th of each month.
New Ship CHEROKEE, 415 tons, Edward Kendrick, Jr. Master.

Clipping from January 1838 Boston newspaper referencing the Cherokee.[5]

Transcription:
This line of Packets have been built to run between the two cities, to sail the 1st and 15th of each month.
New Ship CHEROKEE, 415 tons, Edward Kendrick, Jr., Master

After her construction in 1838, she plied the waters off the east coast between Boston and New Orleans, serving all ports in between.

On January 30, 1846, she found herself sailing, not in the deep waters of the Atlantic, but in tow behind the steamer *Alton,* heading upstream through the Mississippi Delta.

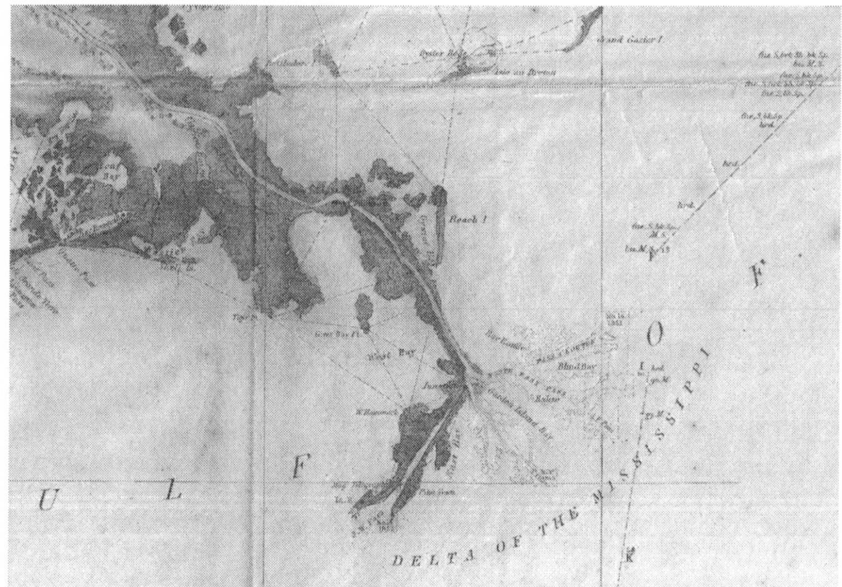

1852 Map of the Mississippi Delta

The ship carried twenty crewmembers and four passengers. At 2:00 a.m. most of the passengers and crew were well asleep, including her commander, Captain Cushing. The only men on duty were the pilot, a mate and the watchman on deck.

A half hour later, something caught the watchman's eye; the bright flickering of flames below deck. As he shouted the alarm, the fire spread rapidly, traveling from the ship's mainmast to the stern – so quickly, in fact, that many of those asleep escaped with nothing "but their night clothes."

The *Cherokee* burned to the waterline over the course of the next nine hours, and finally sunk. Thanks to the watchmen's warning, all aboard were able to escape. However, the only items salvaged were a chest and a writing desk.

The cause of the fire was later attributed to spontaneous combustion.

The survivors were eventually taken to New Orleans, where about twenty of the crew sought a vessel to carry them back to Boston. Unable to find one, they read of a vessel that would soon be sailing for New York. Close enough to Boston, they agreed. In New York they would have their pick from the many Boston-bound ships in port.

This group of sailors would later join Captain Babcock and mate Nicholas Baker aboard the ill-fated *John Minturn*.

1845

British "Penny Red", circa 1845

By the close of 1845, the United States had made great strides in the world of politics, education, culture and science.

On the political front, America had witnessed the passing of its seventh president, Andrew Jackson, who died at the Hermitage, his Tennessee plantation, on June 8.

The current president was James Polk, who had ambitious plans for the country's expansion.

In October 1845, the citizens of the Republic of Texas voted to approve a proposed constitution, which, if approved by Congress, would make Texas the 28th state. It was brought before both Houses and approved on December 29:

A bill for the admission of the State of Texas into the Union.

Whereas the people of Texas have, through their deputies in convention assembled, agreed to the terms and conditions of the joint resolutions of congress, approved March 1, 1845, providing for annexing Texas to the United States; and whereas the said people of Texas have also, by their said deputies in convention, adopted a republican form of government, by forming a constitution, agreeable to the requirements of said joint resolutions; and whereas the same, together with the conditions of annexation, have been ratified by said people of Texas by their vote at the polls:

Be it therefore enacted by the senate and house of representatives of the United States in congress assembled, That the republic of Texas be, and the same is hereby, admitted as a State into the Union, on an equal footing with the original United States, in all respects whatever; and that from and after the passage of this act, the civil and military jurisdiction of the United States government be extended over the said State of Texas.[6]

The addition of Texas as a state was part of Polk's larger policy of expanding aggressively into the West.

As if on cue, Brigham Young departed from Nauvoo, Illinois, with a large contingent of Mormons, and headed due west towards the Great Salt Lake. Here the Church of Jesus Christ of Latter-day Saints would settle in what was then a Mexican territory, which would eventually become the state of Utah.

And the U.S. was not only expanding its geographic borders. By establishing the Naval School in Annapolis, Maryland, it was also increasing its military might. The facility opened on October 10, 1845, and its beginnings were humble: only fifty students and seven professors comprised the first-year class. It would later become the United States Naval Academy.

U.S. Military Academy 1853 ⁷

On the cultural front, one American icon had passed and an American pastime was just getting its start.

Jonathan Chapman, better known as Johnny Appleseed, died on March 18, 1845. He was a pioneering nurseryman who introduced apples to many northern states, including Pennsylvania, Indiana, Ohio and Illinois. Upon his death, Chapman bequeathed to his sister a 1,200 acre estate. He also owned four plots in Allen County, Indiana, including a nursery in Milan Township, with 15,000 trees.

JOHNNY APPLESEED.

Apart from orchards, another field was being used in a radically different way. On October 21, the *New York Herald* became the first newspaper to mention the game of baseball. The following day, the *New York Morning News* included a box score from a baseball game.

Box Score from the *New York Morning News*

The game was played between the Knickerbockers and the Excelsiors at Elysian Fields in Hoboken, New Jersey, across from New York City. The Excelsiors won by a score of 46 to 34.

While the U.S. was expanding its territories, growing its military capabilities and introducing a new sport, many of the period's significant scientific discoveries originated in far-off England.

Up to 1845, Uranus was the furthest-known planet in the solar system. That changed when John Couch Adams, a young British college fellow, completed some math in 1843 that indicated another planet was affecting the orbit of Uranus. This would turn out to be Neptune. Visual confirmation would come later in 1846.

Although this astronomical advance was noteworthy, contemporary understanding about the rest of the solar system lagged behind. Some believed that the Sun was made of coal, while others conjectured that Mars was inhabitable.

But more practical applications of science were also being demonstrated. The British scientist, Michael Faraday, was contributing to the study of electromagnetism and electrochemistry. His main discoveries included the principles underlying electromagnetic induction, diamagnetism and electrolysis. These findings eventually served as the basis for the electric motor.

But it took a devastating fire in Pittsburgh, Pennsylvania, to introduce a major change in engineering in the United States.

The Pittsburg Fire.—By a diagram of the city it appears that full one third, on the Monongahela side, was burnt over—a mile and a quarter, containing 60 acres. Of the 1200 houses estimated as the number lost, about 700 were dwellings, and at least 4000 persons have been thrown out of house and home. Mrs Brooks was burnt in her house in Third street, and two men were missing. The post office and adjoining buildings were saved. The losses of some individuals and houses are from $5000 up to $200,000. One firm of wholesale grocers, the heaviest holders of sugar, molasses, &c., in the city, and also owners of the buildings in which they did business, cannot have lost less than $80 to $100,000. The Monongahela bridge, which cost $110,000, the Monongahela House, which cost $200,000, with its furniture, and the University, are all destroyed. Only about $15,000 was insured in other cities, and of course the Pittsburg offices are great sufferers. The Firemen's Co. loss is $249,000;

Boston Post **clipping describing the fire at Pittsburg** [9]

Transcription:

The Pittsburgh Fire-By a diagram of this city it appears that full one third, on the Monongahela side, was burnt over– a mile and a quarter, containing 60 acres. Of the 1200 houses estimated as the number lost, about 700 where dwellings, and at least 4000 persons had been thrown out of house and home. Mrs. Brooks was burnt in her house in Third Street, and two men were missing. The post office and adjoining buildings were saved. The losses of some individuals and houses are from $5,000 up to $200,000. One firm of wholesale grocers, the heaviest holders of sugar, molasses, &c in the city, and also owners of the buildings in which they did business, cannot have lost less than $80 to $100,000. The Monongahela bridge, which cost $110,000, the Monongahela House, which cost $200,000, with its furniture, and the University, are all destroyed. Only about $15,000 *was insured in other cities, and of course the Pittsburgh offices are great sufferers. The Firemen's Co. loss is $249,000.*

After the flames had completely destroyed the bridge's deck, the only infrastructure undamaged was the piers and abutments.

Fortunately, the partial destruction provided the opportunity to fundamentally change the way bridges were to be constructed in the U.S.

[10]

A 1845 James Baillie print *Great Conflagration at Pittsburgh, PA*. The bridge appears on the bottom right side of the image.

An architect named John Roebling now took advantage of the situation and attempted to rebuild the bridge's eight sections, which spanned 1,500 feet.

11

John Roebling

Roebling's radical idea was to suspend each section of the bridge by two cables from large cast-iron towers atop each pier. He began his work in June 1845. Two cables ran through pendulums at the top of each tower, a revolutionary design at the time. It was called a "wire suspension bridge". His innovative new bridge opened to traffic in February 1846.

12

Roebling's new "Wire Bridge"

According to the *Boston Post*, the opening of the bridge was a great success:

Pittsburgh Wire Bridge.

The "new wire suspension bridge" across the Monongahela, at Pittsburgh, was thrown open to the public on Saturday last. The Gazette says:

"A large number of wagons of all sizes crossed during the day—some of them heavily loaded. Mr. R. contracted to make the bridge as *stiff* as any of the wooden bridges across the Alleghany, and with as little vibration. As two of the latter are new, and constructed upon the most approved principles of modern bridge engineering, this contract was thought by many to be rather a hazardous undertaking, but it is completely successful.—What is most singular, the vibration caused by a number of foot passengers is much greater than that produced by a heavily loaded wagon—at the utmost, it is very slight."

Clipping from the *Boston Post*, January 1846. [13]

Transcription:

The "new wire suspension bridge" across the Monongahela, at Pittsburgh, was thrown open to the public on Saturday last. The Gazette says:

A large number of wagons of all sizes crossed during the day–some of them heavily loaded. Mr. R(oebling) contracted to make the bridge as stiff as any of the wooden bridges across the Allegheny, and with as little vibration. As two of the latter are new, and constructed upon the most approved principles of modern bridge engineering, this contract was thought by many to be rather a hazardous undertaking, but it is completely successful.–What is more singular, the vibration caused by a number of foot passengers is much greater than that produced by a heavily loaded wagon– at the utmost, it is very slight.

Far from the Monongahela River, technology was also advancing in the world of maritime transportation. On August 10, the iron steamship, *Great Britain,* became the first screw-propelled vessel to traverse the Atlantic, completing the voyage from Liverpool to New York in 15 days.

CORRESPONDENCE OF THE BOSTON POST.

New York, Aug. 10th.

Early yesterday morning, the good people of New York, in clubs of hundreds, if not thousands, were found on the Battery, eagerly stretching their eyes to catch a glance at the mammoth steamer, the Great Britain. Patiently they waited till 12 o'clock, when it was announced by telegraph that the monster was in the offing. A thrill of excitement now possessed the multitude, and spy-glasses and telescopes, opera glasses and spectacles, besides all the *glasses* at the Battery Hotel, and at Peter Bayard's Battery House, were in busy requisition. Never, I fancy, were so many *glasses* employed on the Sabbath as there were yesterday.

Whilst the excitement was raging at its utmost, a wag possessed himself of a spy-glass *cane*, minus glasses, which he now and then placed to his eye, and gazed, as he said, at the steamer. He could see her *very* distinctly. Of course all hands were anxious to look through the magical telescope, and each one struggled with the other for the first favor. The *dupe* instantly recognized the hoax, but winked and said nothing, till nineteen twentieths of the multitude were most signally and good naturedly humbugged! One gentleman, however, in green specs and moreen strapped pants, took the high dudgeon, and was for a fight. He was accommodated by a sailor, who defended the "wonderful spy glass," and got a pair of black eyes for his importunity and pains.

By the time the Great Britain had reached the Great Western pier, her news was published in extra sheets by the newspapers, and sent to all parts of the Union. In consequence of the excitement produced by the arrival of the Great Britain, almost all the churches were deserted—a strong comment and certain on the depth of New York piety. 14

The Great Britain

The *Great Britain's* arrival heralded the demise of the age of commercial sail.

But, for the moment, sailing ships would still depend more on manpower than horsepower. Muscle and tendon were needed to tame the ocean's wind and waves. But sometimes the Atlantic would prove to be just too wild and vicious to be sailed upon, no matter the source of a ship's power.

The Pilots

When the ocean-worn bark nears the covered shore,
How welcome the boat with its snowy white wings,
Which comes to assure us the voyage is o'er,
And dove-like the Pilot an olive leaf brings,

How merry the ring of his loud "Ship-a-hoy" ,
How thrills every heart with his tidings of home;
As he bids the sail swell -swell our bosoms with joy,
And sparkle our spirits as sparkles the foam.

And when 'mid the rage of the pitiless storm,
The minute gun's pealing our knell o'er the wave,
How beams every eye as the valorous form
Of the Pilot appears in the life-boat to save.

Brave, generous Pilot, though rugged the way

Amid the fierce surges and storms of the deep,

Ten thousand warm bosoms shall gratefully pray,

That Heaven in safety thy pinnace may keep.

And at last when, thy voyage of life being o'er,

Thy tempest-toss'd bark seeks a haven of rest,

Be an angel thy pilot, and guide to the shore,

Where all who delighted in blessing are blessed. [15]

The following 1845 chart of New York Harbor appears much like it does today.

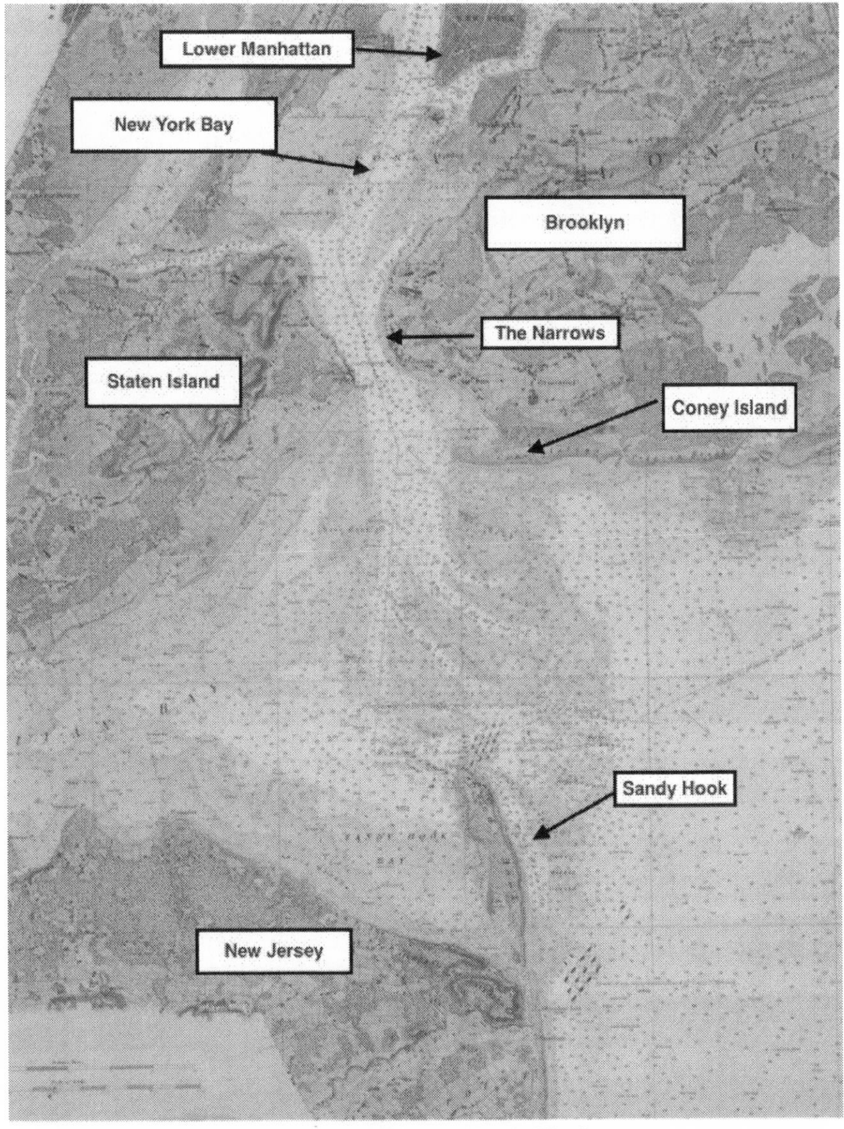

1845 Map of New York Harbor

From the north, the bay receives the freshwater contributions of the Hudson and East rivers; to the south it meets the tidal influences of the Atlantic Ocean.

South of the bay, the waters are pinched by the landmasses of Staten Island on the west and Brooklyn to the east; the currents wend through the gap called the Narrows, the location of today's Verrazano Narrows Bridge.

From that point the land parts, opening into the mouth of the harbor, with Long Island to the east and New Jersey to the south. The topography conjures up the image of an hourglass, which is appropriate considering the vast amount of silt and sand that passes through it on a daily basis. But this simple description belies the dangers that lurk just beneath the calm surface of the harbor's entrance.

As one approaches the Narrows from the south, the depths vary significantly, as seen in a close-up view of the same 1845 map. If a ship can locate the channel, in places, the depth is over 100 feet. But should it stray off course just a little to the east or west, it might find itself run aground in "fine grain sand."

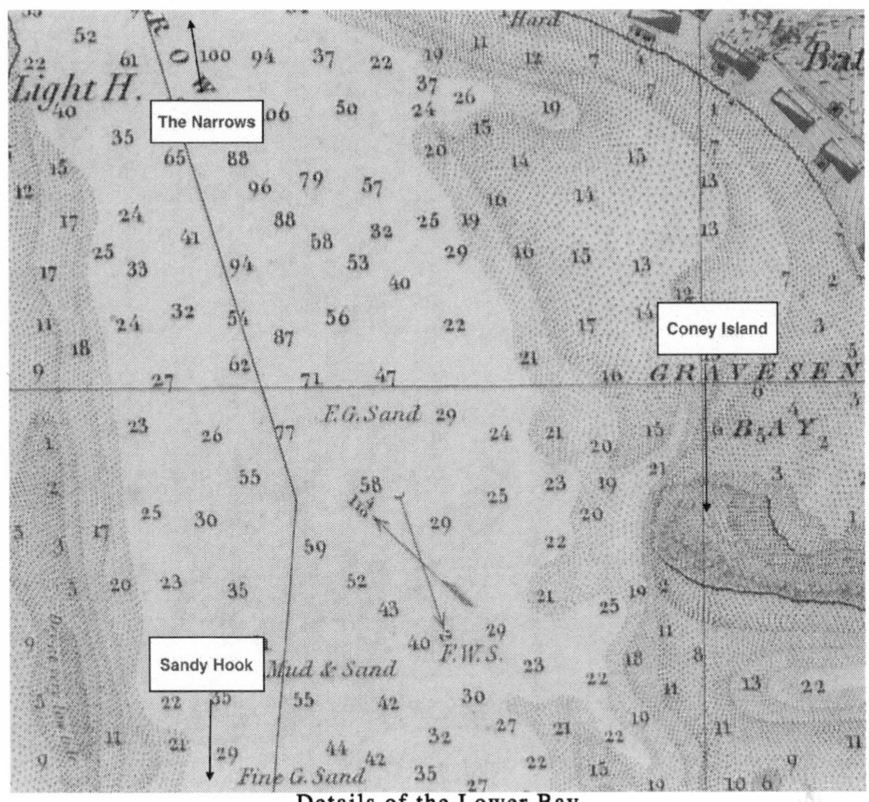

Details of the Lower Bay

A little further south of Coney Island, an even more dangerous situation presents itself. A ship's commander must thread a nautical needle to stay within the tight confines of the channel, a task made more difficult because the channel doesn't align directly with the harbor's north-south orientation, but meanders in a more northwesterly direction.

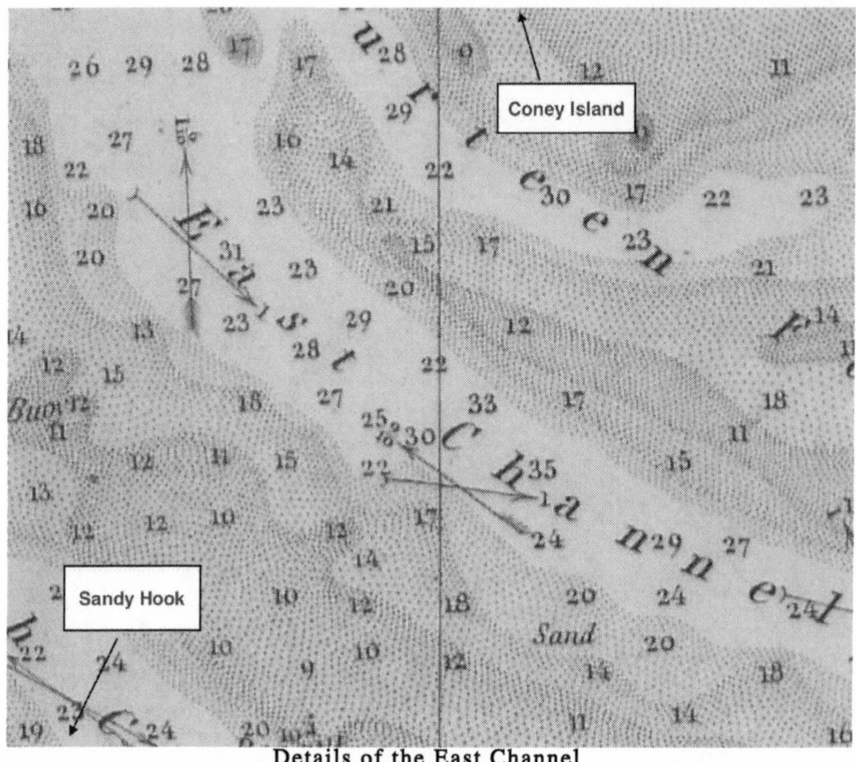

Details of the East Channel

And off the tip of New Jersey's Sandy Hook, further challenges await the mariner. If you mistakenly follow the channel close to shore, you will find yourself crossing over the "False Hook" – a precarious place, especially at low tide. To the east, you may encounter the "Oil Spot"; with a depth of only 10 feet, it is certain to snare any heavily-laden vessel that unwittingly attempts to pass over it.

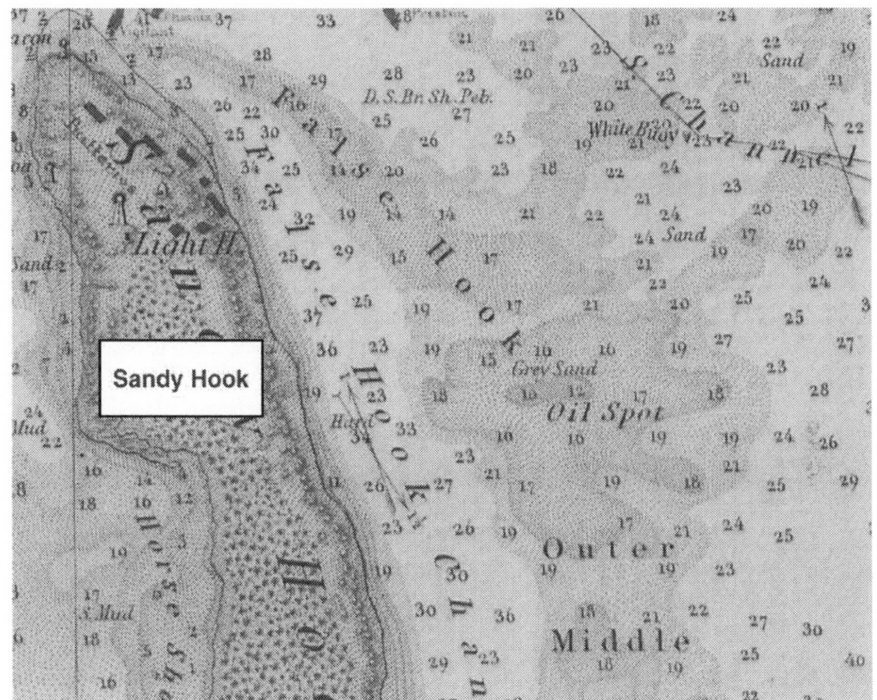

Details of Sandy Hook

As one contemporary mariner described the overall entrance to the harbor:

A glance at a chart of the approaches to New York Harbor reveals that shaping up for its entrance in a sailing vessel in anything other than fair weather can be extremely dangerous. For a hundred miles in either direction, the harbor entrance represents the only serious shelter available to ships of any size.

Then, as now, maneuvering through these waters requires specialized local knowledge; knowledge that must be constantly updated, as the sands shift due to the frequent storms and as new wrecks are added to the list of causalities. Periodic fogs also enter into an already complicated navigational equation.

A hundred and fifty years ago the key to securing passage through these waters was the homegrown group of pilots who were skilled in hydrography and able to plot a course for any type of vessel.

Over the seventeenth century as populations increased, pilotage became a more local profession. The need for local knowledge of tides, currents, shoals, and navigational hazards prompted the change. On March 9, 1694 legislation passed by the Colony of New York appointed the first local mariners as Sandy Hook Pilots.

Before 1836, the licensing of pilots was not uniform. Any individual could obtain a license and represent himself as such, even if they lacked the requisite skills. As an example, one observer noted:

In the years leading up to 1836, pilotage in New York had degenerated into a state of "chaos and slop" with an "every man for himself" attitude holding sway. According to more than one authority, potentially lucrative pilot licenses were increasingly granted to men with political interests who "did not know a ship's keel from a staysail". These political "heelers" based their time at hostelries while so-called apprentices went sea to do their work for them. Some of the apprentices knew little more than their masters of the business to which they were called, so life and death aboard ships approaching this treacherous coast grew more and more chancy. Sometimes, the few honest pilots still in service would be elsewhere when a ship arrived and no pilot was forthcoming.

Despite these observations, the pilots continued to do business. But it required twin 1836 tragedies to call attention to these deficiencies.

In that year, the immigrant ships, the *Mexico* and the *Bristol,* were lost. The two crossed the entire Atlantic uneventfully and were anchored off Sandy Hook, less than a dozen miles from docking in the harbor. Seeking a pilot to escort them, the ships displayed the customary signal and fired their guns.

Despite the call for assistance, not one pilot boat responded from either the New York or New Jersey quarter.

Later, a vicious storm found both ships and drove them onto the beaches of Long Island. Over 200 lives were lost.

LOSS OF THE MEXICO, CAPTAIN WINSLOW, OCTOBER 30, 1836.

Image of the *Mexico*

The resulting outrage led to a New York County investigation:

The Grand Jury are compelled to state that, without exception, the testimony of every merchant and shipowner examined by them was such as to reflect discredit upon the vigilance and activity of the pilots of the City of New York...
It seems to be the inevitable result of a system which selects so small a number for so great a work and which secures, by legislative provisions of the strictest character, the exclusive enjoyment of the offices and in certain cases giving them a moiety of the compensation when no service is performed.
And to the combination alluded above, the greatest portion of the existing evils may be fairly attributed, for being sure of a proportion of the entire income of their profession, the indolent and the dissipated are placed on a footing with the enterprising and moral and every excitement to emulation is completely paralyzed.[16]

Officials from New Jersey and New York responded, although with two markedly different results. The New Jersey Pilots, viewed as more professional and less influenced by political favors, established the Commission of Pilotage. The commission created standards before licensing could be granted. There was a requirement for a pilot to pass a "searching examination" and produce good character references. These requirements further bolstered the group's reputation and many mariners considered them the pilots of choice.

The first pilot licensed by the New Jersey Commission was Theopholis Beebe, who would remain on the list for many years afterwards.

On the New York side, there was some improvement in the quality of the pilots, but things still had political overtones. The officers of an oversight board were appointed by the governor "which continued to leave pilots' licenses open to potential corruption as a political perquisite".

Then, in 1845, the year before the *Minturn* storm, the New York Legislature reversed itself and threw things into complete disarray by repealing all existing piloting regulations:

> **CHAPTER XI.**
>
> **PILOTS AND PILOTAGE**
>
> ***Of the Port of New York.***
>
> **The Legislature of the State of New York, on the 1st of April 1845, passed the following act repealing all former acts in relation to the pilots by the way of Sandy Hook.**
>
> **§ 1. "All laws and parts of laws relative to pilots or pilotage of the port of New York, by the way of Sandy Hook, are hereby repealed: Provided, however, that all persons holding licenses as such pilots on the tenth day of March, eighteen hundred and forty-five, shall be and continue to be pilots by the way of Sandy Hook; but nothing herein contained shall be held to prohibit other persons from acting as such pilots"—*Law* 1845, *p*. 30.**
>
> **From this act it will appear that any person may now exercise the duties of a pilot by the way of Sandy Hook.**

[17]

With the statute overturned, the quality of a New York pilot was again put into question. The absence of regulation now introduced fierce competition between the two rival groups. This again added to the perception that the New York pilots were unqualified.

At the beginning of 1846 there were only thirteen New York registered pilot boats. One of these boats was the *Blossom,* and one of her pilots was a man by the name of Thomas Freeborn. In 1846 he would bring great renown to the New York pilots, but it would come at a tremendous cost.

The *John Minturn*

The *John Minturn* was built in 1841 in Westerly, Rhode Island, just west of the mouth of Narragansett Bay. Westerly was founded by John Babcock, who may have been a relative of Joseph Babcock, the unfortunate captain of the *Van Buren* that was lost on the Aransas Bar in 1845.[18]

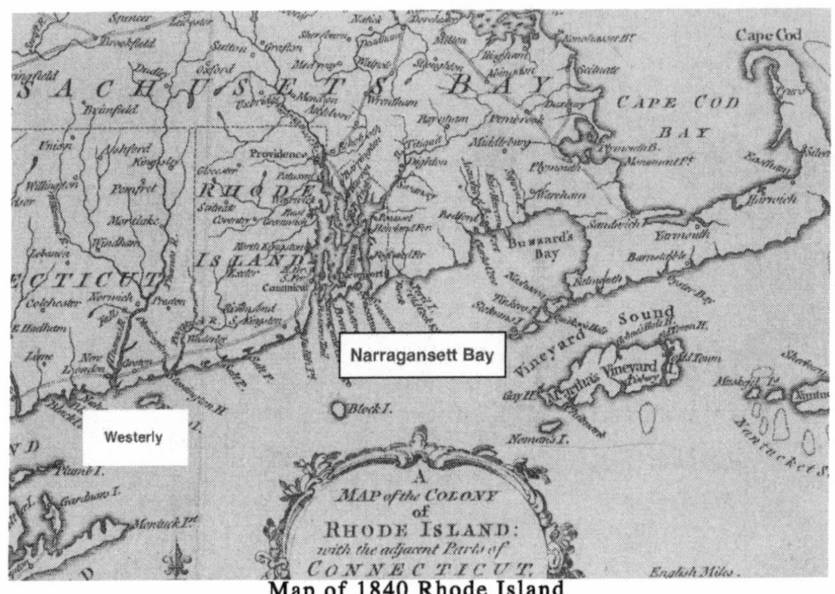

Map of 1840 Rhode Island

The *John Minturn* was a substantial vessel: three-masted, 119 feet in length, a berth of 27 feet, 2 inches and tonnage of 398 75/95. She was registered as being in the "coasting trade" and her homeport was listed as Mystic, Connecticut.

The origin of the ship's name is unclear. There was a wealthy New Yorker by that name who, in 1841, with another person, was "principally interested" in the purchase of the Merchants Bank of New Orleans. Beyond that fact, the genesis of the ship's name is left to conjecture.

More construction details are found in her 1841 New London, Connecticut registration:

NO. 65

ENROLLMENT. In conformity to an Act of the Congress of the United States of America, entitled, "An Act for enrolling and licensing ships, or vessels to be employed in the Coasting trade and Fisheries, and for regulating the same," Dudley Stark and Charles P. Williams of Stonington in the State of Connecticut having taken or subscribed the Oath required by the said act, and having sworn that they together with Charles Mallory and Elisha Faxon of No. Stonington and George E. Allen of the City, County and State of New York, are citizens of the UNITED STATES, and sole owners of the ship or vessel called the John Minturn of Mystic whereof Dudley Stark is at present Master, and as he hath sworn, is a citizen of the UNITED STATES, and that the said ship or vessel was built at Westerly in the State of Rhode Island in the year eighteen hundred and forty one, the present year, as appears by the certificate of Silas Greenman Jr. Master Carpenter under whose direction she was built. And John [illegible] Surveyor of the Port of New London having certified that the said ship or vessel has two decks three masts, and that her length is one hundred nineteen feet one inches; her breadth twenty seven feet two inches; her depth half her breadth feet inches; and that she measures three hundred and ninety eight 75/95 tons, that she is a Ship has a square stern, no galleries and a billet head, and the said Dudley Stark having agreed to the description and admeasurement above specified, and sufficient security having been given according to the said Act, the said Ship has been duly enrolled at the Port of NEW-LONDON.

Given under my Hand and Seal, at the Port of New-London, this 9th day of October in the year One Thousand Eight Hundred and Forty one.

The *John Minturn's* registration

Transcription:

No. 65
Enrollment. In conformity to an Act of Congress of the United States of America, entitled, "An Act for enrolling and licensing ships, or vessels, to be employed in the Coasting trade and Fisheries, and for regulating the same," Dudley Stark and Charles P. Williams of Stonington, in the State of Connecticut, having taken or subscribed the Oath required by the said act, having sworn that they together with Charles Mallory and Elisha Faxon of Stonington and George L. Meacham of the city, county and state of New York are citizens of the United States and sole owners of the ship or vessel called the John Minturn of Mystic whereof Dudley Stark is at present Master, and as he hath sworn, is a citizen of the United States, and that the said ship or vessel was built at Westerly in the State of Rhode Island in the year eighteen hundred and forty one, this present year as appears by the certificate of Silas Greenman as Master Carpenter, under whose direction she was built and John Frank (illegible) of the Port of New London having certified that the said ship or vessel has two decks, three masts and that her length is One hundred nineteen feet no inches; her breadth twenty seven feet , two inches; her depth half her breadth feet - inches and that she measures Three hundred and ninety eight 75/95 tons, that she is a Ship - has a square stern, no galleries and a Billet head and that said Dudley Stark, having agreed to the description and measurements above specified, and sufficient security having been given according to said act, the said Ship has been duly enrolled in the City at the Port of New London.
Given under my Hand and Seal, at the Port of New London, this 9th day of October in the year One Thousand Eight Hundred and Forty one.

The master carpenter listed was Silas Greenman, Jr., who with his brother George, had learned the trade from their father, Silas Greenman, when they worked in Mystic, Connecticut in the 1830s and 1840s. The two brothers worked in partnership until 1835, when Silas Jr. decided to move the business south to Westerly. There he built larger ships, including the *John Minturn*.

Although the document details some of her physical dimensions, it lacks other information that provides a picture of how she actually appeared.

The "Billet Head" mentioned in the document refers to the addition of a decorative piece at the forefront of the ship; it would have looked something like this:

This was more modest than the larger carved wooden figureheads that appeared on other vessels:

According to one source, the ship was painted "bottle green with a white stripe." And curiously, it had thirteen simulated "gun ports" painted on both sides of the hull.[19] It is unknown whether the purpose was decorative or intended to ward off coastal pirates.

The only image known of the *John Minturn* is an 1846 lithograph by Currier and Ives, showing the vessel in her death throes.

The Currier and Ives painting of the *John Minturn*

The thirteen painted-in gun ports can be clearly seen across the white stripe. The contrast of the dark against the white border would have made them stand out at a great distance.

After the *John Minturn's* formal registration on October 9, 1841, she was soon placed into service. On October 19, after a two-day trip from Connecticut, she arrived in New York Harbor. Sometime that fall, the *Minturn* made her maiden voyage to New Orleans.

Around January 21, 1842, she returned from New Orleans carrying a load of flour, arriving in New York after a trip of only 13 days. The speed of her voyage must have pleased both her captain and owners. According to one report, under full sail she could "plow through high seas at 12 knots."

From 1842 to 1844 she ran routine voyages between New York and New Orleans, completing at least five trips in 1842, seven in 1843 and eight in 1844.

The ship carried mostly commercial products. In a representative 1843 trip to New York she delivered the following:

- 42 hhds (hogshead barrels) tobacco
- 200 bbl (barrels) of molasses
- 281 bales of cotton
- 37 hhds of sugar
- 4995 pig lead
- 500 sks corn
- 37 bales of rope
- 25 bales of cotton to order

Although she principally transported cargo, she also carried passengers. On the front page of the January 19, 1844 edition of the *New York Daily Tribune*, the following advertisement appeared:

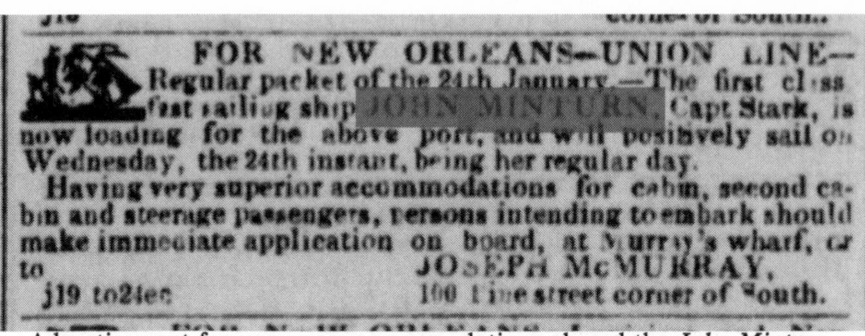
FOR NEW ORLEANS—UNION LINE—Regular packet of the 24th January.—The first class fast sailing ship JOHN MINTURN, Capt Stark, is now loading for the above port, and will positively sail on Wednesday, the 24th instant, being her regular day.

Having very superior accommodations for cabin, second cabin and steerage passengers, persons intending to embark should make immediate application on board, at Murray's wharf, or to

JOSEPH McMURRAY,

j19 to24ec 100 Pine street corner of South.

Advertisement for passenger accommodations aboard the *John Minturn*

Transcription:

For New Orleans-Union Line-
Regular packet of the 24th January-The first class fast sailing ship JOHN MINTURN, Capt. Stark, is now loading for the above port, and will positively sail on Wednesday, the 24th instant, being her regular day.
Having very superior accommodations for cabin, second cabin and steerage passengers, persons intending to embark should make immediate application on board, at Murray's wharf, or to
Joseph McMurray
100 Pine street corner of South

For this particular voyage, she also carried some very important passengers, at least from the captain's viewpoint. In a March 1843 trip to New Orleans, fifteen passengers accompanied Captain Stark:

Passengers Arrived.

London—Packet ship Ontario—F I Stephenson, E Bannister, Philadelphia; Madame Berniss, Paris; J Young, London—12 in steerage.

Hamburg—Barque Washington—Mr Ahrenburg, and 9 in the steerage.

New Orleans—Ship John Minturn—Mrs Peck and child, Mrs and Miss Stark, W B Hull, D D Mallory—and 9 in the steerage.

At Boston—In the Columbia, from Liverpool—Rt Hon Sir

Listing of passengers arriving in New Orleans aboard the *John Minturn*

Transcription:
New Orleans-Ship John Minturn-Mrs Peck and child. Mrs and Miss Stark, W.B. Hull, D D Mallory- and 9 in the steerage

The Mrs. Stark mentioned was Captain Stark's wife, Catherine. The two had married on November 4, 1822 in Stonington, 21 years earlier. She was Stark's junior by 18 years; he was 48 at the time of the voyage to New Orleans, she 30.

Joining the couple on the voyage to New Orleans was their nine-year old daughter, Helen (listed as "Miss Stark"). The couple's son, Stephen, is notably absent from the listing and may have accompanied his father on another voyage to New Orleans.

In 1846, the three family members would board the *John Minturn* with the captain for a return trip from New Orleans, presumably to their home in Stonington, Connecticut, via New York.

During the *Minturn's* brief life, she enjoyed some commercial success. However, there were a few setbacks, some minor, some more serious.

In September 1842, one of the Minturn's passengers, Paul Patterson, was robbed of $340 in doubloons and silver, reportedly while aboard the ship. An indictment of grand larceny was brought against a fellow passenger David Lewis, but he absconded to Canada with his loot. The account was reported in several newspapers.

In March 1844, the *Minturn* found herself referenced in the newspaper again, this time as a result of an unfortunate accident that was not her fault. She was berthed along a New York wharf when another vessel, the *Texidor,* was attempting to come alongside. A *Texidor* boatman by the name of John Dunivan slipped off the deck and was crushed between the two vessels. He died soon afterwards.

But the most serious incident took place at sea in October 1843. The *Minturn* departed New Orleans, carrying a cargo of cotton and tobacco. At latitude 28, longitude 79 1/2, off the east coast of Florida, she encountered a vicious storm. The damage to the *Minturn* was significant. She lost her "fore topmast, foretop-gallant mast, main topgallant, and main royalmast" and the storm also did "other damage". The *Minturn* limped into New York Harbor in October, taking twenty-seven days on a journey that she had once completed in thirteen.

The 1843 experience was notable because it gave the *John Minturn* her first taste of a life-threatening storm. The next encounter would be far more challenging.

Undiminished Violence

He who foresees calamities, suffers them twice over--Porteus

In 1846, the residents of the east coast of the United States understood that a great storm was overdue. The previous year the Atlantic hurricane season had been quiescent – not one tropical storm or hurricane was recorded.

This was also reflected in the scant number of shipwrecks off the New Jersey coast found in the following graph.

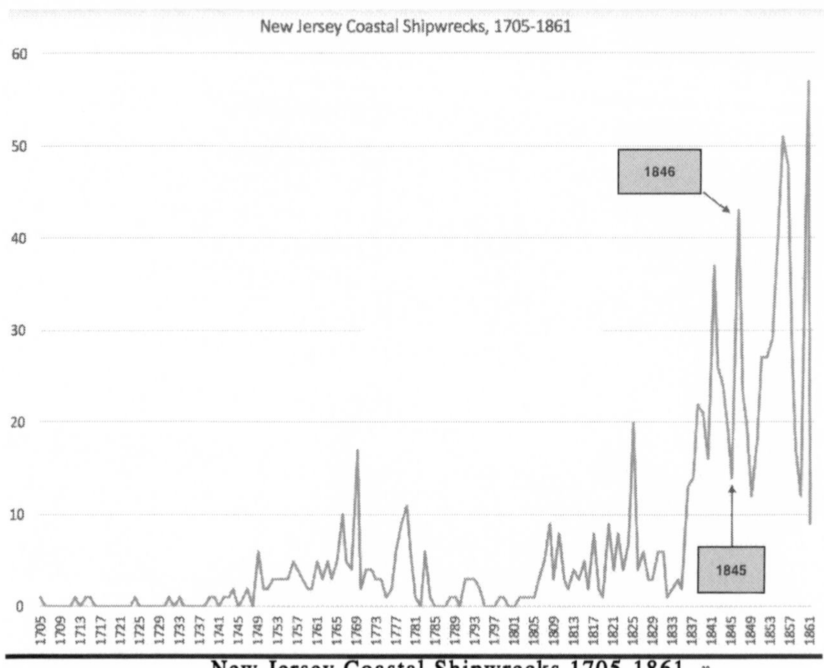

New Jersey Coastal Shipwrecks 1705-1861 [20]

The 1845 calm represented a significant change from previous years. Between 1840 and 1844, a total of seven tropical storms and twelve hurricanes roared into the Atlantic, causing widespread shipping losses.

The most significant of these storms was the October 1841 hurricane that struck New England, causing massive damage, particularly in Connecticut and Massachusetts. Snowdrifts of up to 18 feet were recorded and over 190 ships were indiscriminately destroyed.[21]

The storm's greatest single calamity was visited upon the small town of Truro, near the eastern tip of Cape Cod. On October 3, a half dozen fishing boats were lost, along with scores of men and boys, some as young as eleven. Today, the graveside memorial reads:

Sacred to the memory of 57 citizens

of Truro who were lost in seven

vessels which foundered at sea in the

memorable gale of October 3, 1841

Then shall the dust return to the

earth as it was and the spirit shall

return unto God who gave it.

Man goeth to his long home and the

mourners go about the street.

With fresh memories of the 1841 gale and storms in 1844, the coastal residents found the 1845 calm unsettling. They often found themselves looking to both the sky and sea for signs of the next great tempest.

Something had to be brewing.

When a powerful storm finally struck the northeast coast in 1846, it came as no great surprise. But what was astonishing was its intensity and reach.

The storm tracked from the south – typical of most nor'easters – and hugged the coastline of the southern states. There were many contemporaneous newspaper accounts reporting its northerly progress.

Georgetown, S.C. :

We have had a very severe gale of wind here this morning, the most so of any that has occurred here within the last six years. We had but two vessels in port, and they rode out the blow in safety. The weather continued to thicken, and the wind became a gale by 10 o'clock and blew with great fury till 12 o'clock, at S.E. and E.S.E. Great damage has been done to the rice field banks and the wharves. Some 2000 or 3000 sticks of timber were put adrift and floated up near the saw mill...Captain March's pilot boat, the Cora, was ran (sic) into by the drifting rafts of timber, carried into the stream and sunk.[22]

Charleston, S.C. :

On Friday afternoon last [Feb13], it commenced raining, and continued throughout the night, with little cessation, the wind in the mean time blowing tolerably fresh.

The appearance of the weather was so unfavorable in the afternoon of Friday, and the sea was running so high on the bar, that the Wilmington mail boat returned, thus fortunately escaping an encounter with the storm, which followed.

About eight o'clock on Saturday morning, the wind increased in violence, and in about half an hour thereafter, it blew with a force truly terrific. There were in the harbor about 70 sail of square rigged vessels, in all possible positions, taking and discharging cargoes, ready for sea...not especially prepared for withstanding a gale, as such a warning of the elements is quite unusual at this season of the year.

Fortunately it was in open day light, and with the promptness and fearlessness characteristic of the hardy sons of the ocean, every precaution that could be taken to withstand the violence of the gale was immediately resorted to. Had it taken place in the course of the night, crowded as the wharves were with craft of every description, the destruction would have been tremendous. As it was, the "scene" was truly awful. At about 10 o'clock, when the gale was at its height, the crashing and grinding of the vessels against each other, and the ripping up of the wharves in many instances- the dashing of the waves, which breaking against whatever obstruction they encountered, sent the salt spray-in messy volumes-high in the air, and in many instances carrying up boards and pieces of wreck...was a spectacle grand but fearful to look upon. [23]

Richmond, Virginia:

We had yesterday an old-fashioned snow storm, commencing about one o'clock, and accompanied with a strong wind. The weather was cold and disagreeable, and it is likely to be so for some days to come.[24]

Philadelphia, Pennsylvania:

About 4 o'clock on Saturday afternoon [Feb14], a storm of snow, rather suddenly visited this city, and after dallying a little while, as if to create hopes that the few shavings that had descended were nearly all that were to come, sent down thick flakes so fast and close together, that in a short time there was a covering upon the ground some three inches deep. The wind rose, too, and blew strongly from the westward, increasing in strength until about three o'clock yesterday morning, when it blew a perfect gale. The wind swept along with terrific force, and sung and whistled in a manner quite unbecoming in a sober latitude like this, committing, as it went, such pranks as will be any thing but pleasant to those who have to repair the damage it occasioned. Among the disasters attended upon the gale, was the uprooting of the venerable Lombardy poplar, which stood in front of the Friends' School, in Fourth, below Chestnut st(reet) . There are associations connected with this time-honored and sombre tree; and it is one of the "Ten Trees" spoken of in Watson's Annals of this city. We have heard that the consequences of the gale are to be seen all over the city, in the prostrated awning post, uprooted trees, signs torn from their fastenings, and other exposed objects. ***There is reason to fear that there has been great destruction along the coast.*** [Emphasis added]

The heavy snow storm of course laid an embargo upon the rail road trains and we were without papers from any quarter until four o'clock in the afternoon, when the southern mail, due at four o'clock yesterday morning, arrived. The violence of the wind was so great that the ferryboat while crossing the Susquehanna river to Havre de Grace, with Philadelphia passengers, was blown across the end of the pier and went aground, where she remained a little more than seven hours-thus occasioning a delay to both lines. About three miles this side of the Susquehanna the snow storm was encountered and three locomotives having been sent with snow ploughs, the train proceeded on until within three miles of this city, where the snow, drifted into a deep cut, resisted the snow ploughs for three hours. The eastern mail arrived about five o'clock, some three hours after the time at which it was due. We understand the most strenuous exertions were made, as soon as the storm came on, to keep the road clear, and between New Brunswick and Bordentown seven locomotives were employed in clearing it by the aid of snow ploughs, and the communication with New York is uninterrupted.[25]

Syracuse, New York:

The whole country is buried beneath an avalanche of snow, which fell from the clouds, principally during the morning of Sunday, the 15th inst. The storm commenced on Saturday evening [Feb. 14], about an hour before midnight; and those who were to attend the railroad trains at 4 o'clock the next morning, state there was then some six inches of snow on the ground. Between that hour and 9 o'clock , the snow fell so rapidly , that it had accumulated to the depth of two feet. A heavier fall of snow within the same time, was never known. After 9 or 10 o'clock, the storm abated and by one had ceased altogether. The entire depth of snow which fell within a period of fourteen hours, was not less than twenty-eight inches, whilst most persons estimate it at two feet and a half. We are told that during the thickest of the storm, after daylight, the snow fell seven inches in an hour and a half! [26]

New York:

The wind, through the afternoon of Saturday [Feb. 14], had been light, and the inward-bound fleet, known to be very large, were crowding every thing to get into our bay. At nine o'clock, it commenced to blow a reefing breeze; it soon made two reefs necessary; close reef quickly followed, and, by eleven o'clock, scarcely any vessel could carry more sail than enough to lie to with. The force of the gale was from E.N.E, but it shifted, for a moment at a time, to every point on the compass. It was impossible to claw off shore; an attempt to scud was to end only in stranding, and lying to was a hopeless effort, and beyond the endurance of canvas, rigging, or spars.[27]

At the Battery, particularly, the force and power of the wind was exhibited in a striking manner. The waves rolling up in a vast volume, beat with tremendous violence against the barricade of stone, and breaking, threw cataracts of water in the street, and flooding not only the street itself some three or four feet deep, but also inundating the yards and gardens of the residents of the west side of the Battery, completely cutting off all communication with the inmates of some of the houses.

A thrilling incident occurred at the Battery at the very commencement of the gale. A canal boat, owned by a Mrs. Swinton, and having three negroes on board, broke adrift, and came down with much force against the stone work, dashing her to pieces in a short time, of course.

Two of the Negroes succeeded in saving themselves, but one aged and paralyzed with fear was unable to help himself.[28]

Boston, Massachusetts :

The greatest snow storm of the season commenced in this vicinity on Sunday morning [Feb.15], about half past five o'clock. Although the weather during the whole of Saturday was moderate, and the wind light from N.W., yet the clouds in the eastward were dark and heavy, indicating the approach of a storm. About mid-night the wind changed to the eastward, and subsequently lulled almost into a calm; but about 5 A.M. it sprung suddenly up, and, in about half an hour, blew with great fury, accompanied with a dense fall of snow. ***The wind continued blowing with undiminished violence, drifting the snow in heaps stories high, until about 3 P.M. when it became squally, with lulls or intervals of***

about five minutes, the snow, however, coming down with intermission. [Emphasis Added][29]

The great snow storm of the season, visited us yesterday, commencing between four and five o'clock in the morning, and continuing with great violence and a strong northerly wind, throughout the day. The snow was drifted badley (sic) and some of the sidewalks of the city are nearly impassable. The barometer fell in twelve hours from 29.95 to 29.15. The railroad tracks are of course all blocked up and a good deal of labor will be required to free them from their heavy encumbrance. The storm probably commenced at the South, and neither the Norwich nor Stonington trains had reached the city when our papers went to press.[30]

Salem, Massachusetts:

An old-fashioned northeast snow storm commenced yesterday morning [Feb.15] and continued with great severity through the day. We have had nothing to equal it since 1831. Our streets and roads completely blocked up and made almost impassable by the huge snowdrifts. The mail train due from Boston did not arrive here– indeed it must have been impossible to make any headway against the storm. Drifts 15 to 20 feet in height are said to be piled up, and the track must be covered to the depth of several feet throughout nearly its whole extent. The gale was very severe, and it must have been a dreadful day for the sailors on the coast.

In every direction, as far as heard from, the storm was very severe. The steamboats on the Sound, and the mails on the railroads, failed of their regular trips, and there is consequently no late news from the South. [31]

New Bedford, Massachusetts:

We were visited on Sunday {Feb. 15] with a regular old-fashioned Northeaster. The storm commenced about daybreak, and continued furiously through the day until 6 P.M. The snow is badly drifted, presenting accumulations in many of our streets, of from four to six feet in height, and the average level is probably not less than two feet. The quantity of snow on the ground is said to be greater than at any time previous in this vicinity since the memorable snowstorm in 1815. The churches were thinly attended, and in several of the services, except in the morning, were deferred. The railroad between this place and Taunton was badly obstructed...[32]

New London, Connecticut (several reports):

Great snow storm–the storm of wind and snow with which our city was visited on Sunday, the 15th, certainly deserves the distinguishing appellation of great- so great a body of snow not having fallen in this section of the country at least anyone time for the last ten years. We judge, to be sure, from a very limited observation, not, at this writing (Monday morning) having had an opportunity to hear the effects of the storm out of the city.

Here the snow is piled in heaps of all the imaginable shapes and dimensions, and in the streets running north and south, this snow lies on the east side to the average depth of five feet, and we have noticed a number of houses where it lies not less than six feet in depth directly against the front doors. Traveling will undoubtedly be very much impeded for some days, and those of our citizens who depend for their supply of milk upon milkmen residing out of the city, we are afraid we'll have to take their coffee without it this morning.[33]

Yesterday afternoon about four o'clock, we were visited by another "north easter" in the shape of a snow storm, which continued this morning. The snow now upon the ground will average eighteen inches-and the mercury down to zero. Whew! Fine times these.[34]

While the reports across cities and towns recorded delays and hardships, the effects at sea were far greater. The concern that "*there*

is reason to fear that there has been great destruction along the coast" would prove to be an accurate prediction.

Virginia:

A report is in circulation here this morning that a ship or bark, name unknown[*]*, is ashore at Chincoteague Island, her crew all dead, except a small boy, with smallpox. I cannot ascertain where from, where bound, or what laden with.*[35]

Boston (several reports):

On Sunday morning [Feb. 15], about 3 o'clock, Capt. Fowler, seeing every indication of a storm, left Nauset and shaped his course for Provincetown. Between 4 and 5 o'clock the storm commenced from the eastward, and about six it blew a perfect hurricane, rendering the surface of the sea white with foam and drifting spray...Fowler says that it was the most severe gale that he had experienced for five years.[36]

---

[*] The ship is most likely the *Democrat*

The brig Eliza Burgess, which arrived here yesterday was running in under double reefed topsails on Sunday when the storm was so dense with snow as to shut out the land, and the first those on board knew of her true position, was from the keeper of Boston Light, who saw her running for sure destruction, and hailed her from the top of the light through a speaking trumpet. Fortunately he was heard- the brig was rounded and anchored, but in such a precarious position that swinging she brought a ledge of rocks between her and the anchor.[37]

A few days since a humpback whale was killed in Provincetown bay by a party of whalers, who sold it for $99. The schooner Abbathula took it in tow on Saturday for the purpose of bringing it to Boston to be exhibited at so much per head, by way of speculation; but unfortunately the schooner was overtaken by the gale of Sunday, and was compelled to cut the whale adrift.[38]

The gale commenced last evening about 8 o'clock, and had aggregated itself to a fury by midnight; and as a heavy fall of snow commenced at the same time. I am fearful that much damage has been done to the fleet of merchantmen that is known to be on the coast. Ay, and I fear that some gallant sailor who was buoyant with hope yesterday, found a watery grave ere the day dawned, and now slumbers with "the sheeted relics of his ancestors" :

Alas! Poor fellow!
Days, months, years and ages shall cycle away,
And still the dread waters above thee shall roll;
Earth loses thy pattern, forever and aye-
Oh, sailor boy, sailor boy, peace to thy soul.

The gale must have been terrific on the eastern coasts of Maine, New Hampshire and Massachusetts, and fears are already entertained for the safety of our commerce in that direction. Such a storm I do not think has been experienced these last twenty years. Few of our churches are open to-day, and those that have "opened wide their gates" are not greeted by extensive congregations.[39]

Schooner Harriet, (of Hull), Mitchell, from Portland via Provincetown, with a cargo of hay and potatoes, for Boston, went ashore Sunday, during the gale, at about 9 o'clock a.m. on Chelsea

Beach, and has gone to pieces. Crew saved themselves by a surf-skiff which fortunately was on board.[40]

Schooner Louisa Beaton, Cushman, of and from New Bedford, for New York with 1000 bbl sp(erm) oil, 20,000 lbs whalebone, went ashore in the snow storm of Sunday last, on the south side of Great Gull Island, and bilged. Captain C(ushing) at New London on Monday, and chartered a number of vessels, which proceeded to the wreck on Tuesday morning. For the purpose of disch'g the freight.

Schooner Harriet, of Hull ...driven ashore on Chelsea Beach, is high and dry, and, together with her cargo, will be nearly a total loss.[41]

A deeply laden brig, iced up to the leading blocks, was also seen yesterday off Plymouth, supposed to be bound to Boston. The ship Sarah, from Mobile, was in the bay on Sunday, and as her fore and main topgallant masts were gone, it is supposed she lost them in the gale.[42]

New York:

Of the twelve New York pilot boats, eleven were at sea during the hurricane, at distances varying from fifty to one hundred miles from land, scudding over the troubled waters, like angels of mercy, ready to conduct the noble ship to a haven of safety. We have not yet received intelligence of the safety of all of them; but if skill and daring are of any avail, those noble and intrepid fellows will all reach port in safety. These are the men who have sustained for years, the malignant attacks of the Wall Street press. These are the men who are daily accused of hugging the shore and creeping under cover at the approach of a storm. In the middle of a severe winter, and in the midst of a gale of almost unexampled violence, we see these men facing almost death itself in the discharge of their duty. Is it not time that the country in general took up their case and did them justice?

The amount of injury thus far ascertained, varies from a quarter to a half million of dollars...The night if the 14th of February, 1846, will long be remembered. [43]

The New York pilot boats – the angels of mercy – would certainly encounter the storm head-on, and one from their ranks would not survive what would later be called the "Minturn Storm".

Mounting Causalities

By the early morning hours of Sunday, February 15, the storm had moved off to the north and west, and in its path left many vessels lying scattered along the New Jersey coast. They ranged in size from smallish pilot boats to 100-ton brigs.

Many of the vessels had embarked from ports in South Carolina, Georgia and Louisiana, and for most their ultimate destination was New York Harbor. Although their point of origin, size and vessel type could distinguish them, they all shared an ongoing battle for life and death as the day began.

If an observer walked from the northern tip of the New Jersey coastline that Sunday morning, they would have encountered wreckage that grew worse as they moved south.

The first victim of the *Minturn* storm revealed herself on Sandy Hook. The "Hook", as it was known locally, is a spit of sand six miles in length extending just south of New York Harbor.

Map of the area around New York Harbor

In 1846, it was a desolate peninsula, connected at its southern end to the New Jersey mainland by a slender thread of sand. Although those on land had little use for the barren strip, it was a most welcome sight for mariners traveling north. It represented journey's end – the last point of land before they entered the great harbor of New York.

However, on this morning, Sandy Hook had captured the New York pilot boat *Mary Ellen*.

Location of the *Mary Ellen*, off Sandy Hook

The *Mary Ellen* had been "fifty or sixty" miles out to sea when she was caught in the clutches of the storm. According to a *New York Herald* report about the *Mary Ellen's* crew:

> *...and having tried every effort that human skill could devise, to keep an offing, finding that they must be stranded, the brave crew boldly determined to put her ashore to the best advantage.*[44]

Fortunately for crew and owners, the encounter was relatively benign. After running the vessel toward the beach, it was driven far enough up the shore to enable the crew to safely slog to safety. The *Mary Ellen* sustained minor damage and was back out to sea just a few days later.

About eleven miles further south stood the small villages of Raccoon Island and Fishtown (present-day North Long Branch and Monmouth Beach, respectively). At the time, they were sparsely populated with a smattering of homes owned by the Wardell, Cook and West families.

While these inhabitants lay sleeping in the early hours of the 15th, they were awakened by the continuous flapping of shingles against the sides of their homes. The wind was so violent that some of the cladding was ripped away and launched like weapons through the air. As the families hunkered down, they were blissfully unaware of the desperate struggle taking place just a short distance from their homesteads.

The *Pioneer*, under the command of Captain Corsen, with a crew of five was transporting corn and meal to New Haven, Connecticut. The schooner had left Philadelphia the day before, and as she struggled north, the storm's easterly winds and tides forced her towards the shore. At 3:00 a.m. the *Pioneer* was caught on a sandbar. Adding to her predicament was her position on the shoals; she was situated broadside to the beach, meaning that every wave that lashed her starboard side swept over her deck and rocked her violently.

Her only good fortune on that stormy morning was her location. She was about 500 yards southeast of the home of Elias West, and it was Elias that discovered the *Pioneer* in the dim light.

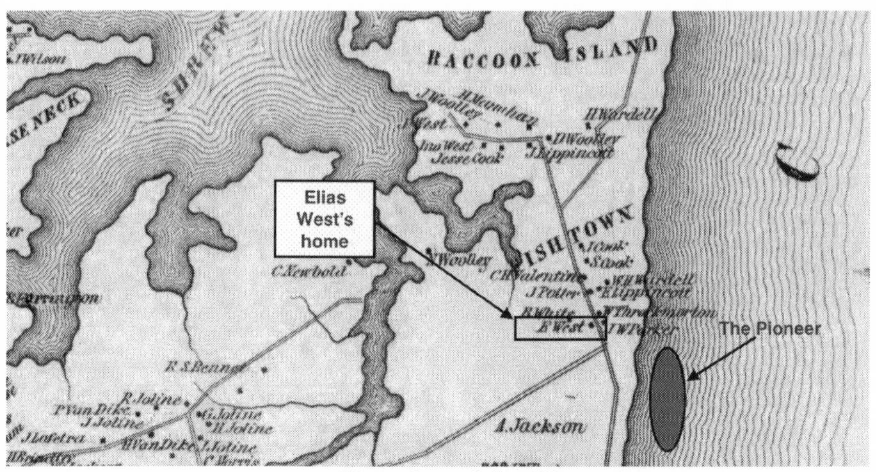

Location of the *Pioneer*

Through the heavy rain and mist, West was able to spot a lone survivor in the vessel's stern. The man was being thrashed with every breaker that rolled over the deck, and his grip appeared to be loosening by the minute. Then West made a startling discovery; a cluster of men was clinging to the ship's rigging, although he could not discern exactly how many.

The vessel's condition was also tenuous as a result of the incessant pounding she was receiving. She could only sustain so much punishment before breaking up. West quickly came to understand that he alone would have to rescue the men, and it had to be done immediately. There was no time to obtain aid from anyone in Fishtown.

He called out to the *Pioneer.* No reply. The pounding waves drowned out all other sounds.

When all seemed lost, the Fates intervened to provide him with a lifeline – literally. The storm's ferocity had severed a rope from the *Pioneer's* rigging, sending it adrift in the surf. The breakers had nudged the line towards shore, where West managed to grab it.

Despite the wind's force, West was able to cast one end into the *Pioneer's* stern, where it was caught by one of the men. West motioned for the man to time his entry into the surf as the vessel pitched towards the shore, and then quickly pulled the man through the surf and up onto the safety of the beach.

Elias West would repeat the operation four more times, single-handedly rescuing the entire crew.

Twelve miles from Sandy Hook and about a mile south of the *Pioneer*, the 100-ton schooner, *Register,* was trapped in the surf. She was under the command of Captain Powers and carried a crew of five and a single passenger. The *Register* was transporting turpentine from the port of New Bern, North Carolina, to New York.

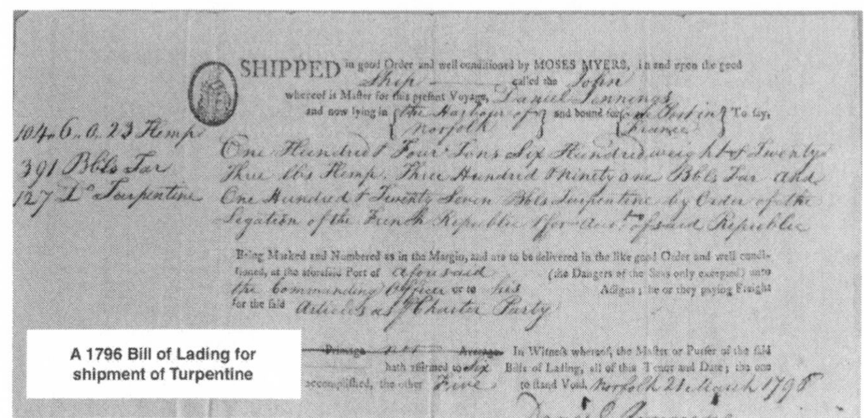

SHIPPED in good Order and well conditioned by MOSES MYERS, in and upon the good Ship called the John whereof is Master for this present Voyage, Daniel Jennings and now lying in the Harbour of Norfolk and bound for France To say,

104.6.0.23 Hemp
391 Bbls Tar
127 Do Turpentine

One Hundred Four Tons Six Hundredweight & Twenty Three lbs Hemp. Three Hundred Ninety one Bbls Tar and One Hundred Twenty Seven Bbls Turpentine by Order of the Legation of the French Republic ... Republic

Being Marked and Numbered as in the Margin, and are to be delivered in the like good Order and well conditioned, at the aforesaid Port of aforesaid (the Dangers of the Seas only excepted) unto the commanding Officer or to his Assigns; he or they paying Freight for the said Articles as pr Charter Party

Primage ... Average. In Witness whereof, the Master or Purser of the said ... hath affirmed to Six Bills of Lading, all of this Tenor and Date; the one accomplished, the other Five to stand Void. Norfolk 21 March 1798

An example of a Bill of Lading

The *Register*, like her neighbor the *Pioneer,* lay parallel to the shore. She was thrashing in an undertow near the Long Branch boarding houses. She was caught on the shoals, two hours after the *Pioneer* at 5:00 a.m.

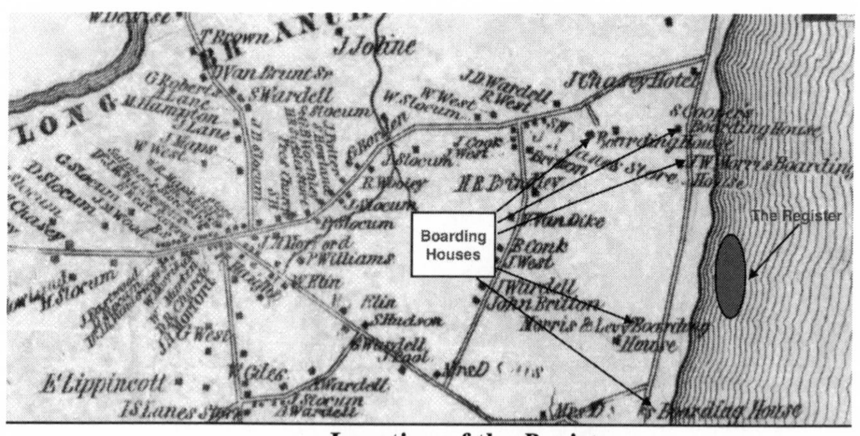

Location of the *Register*

Unlike the *Pioneer*, she had better luck maneuvering through the treacherous sandbars and was able to drive herself close enough to shore, allowing one of her crew to swim ashore. The frigid sailor ran up the beach and arrived at the doorstep of Jacob W. Morris. A startled Morris realized the urgency of the situation and enlisted the help of a neighbor, Charles Bennett. The three men rushed to the wreck site.

It was 5:30 a.m.

When they arrived, they found the *Register* swinging violently in the shore break, in sync with the ebb and flow of the waves. Because she was so near the beach, her masts "were dashing up and down the sands of the shore". Through the dim light the three men on shore could barely see survivors; two men were in the surf holding onto the vessel while two others clung to the mainmast.

Morris and Bennett then worked to retrieve the men from the surf, then followed up by rescuing the other two. Their efforts were timely. At 6:00 a.m., just thirty minutes after their arrival, the *Register* disintegrated, scattering her remains along the shoreline.

However, the *Register's* story was not entirely a success. Before Morris and Bennett's arrival, an unnamed passenger was lost and never found. The *Minturn* storm had claimed its first victim.

Given the storm's continued fury, the expectation grew that the death toll would rise as one proceeded further south.

The *Arkansas,* a Boston-bound schooner was discovered three miles further south. It was manned by a crew of seven and carried a shipment of corn. When the storm caught her at 3:00 a.m., she was heading towards shore, and a young crewman fell overboard, and was lost.

The *Arkansas* was positioned precariously in the combers off the town of Deal, directly opposite the home of Thomas T. Borden.

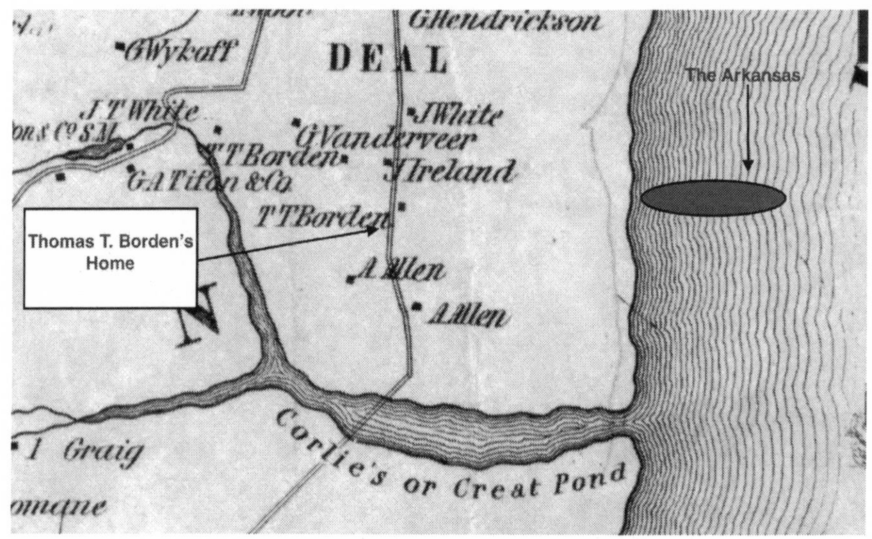

Location of the *Arkansas*

Two town residents, Charles McGinty and Cornelius Brown, ventured from their homes at 6:00 a.m. to investigate the storm. McGinty and Brown's curiosity would prove to be a godsend for the men aboard the *Arkansas.*

Through the blinding snow, the men saw the *Arkansas*'s crew clinging desperately to the rigging. At the crest of each wave, the ocean appeared to be clutching at the men's boots.

McGinty and Brown made visual contact with the crew and motioned for the sailors to "walk" across the jib boom and get closer to shore. The crew followed the directions, and McGinty and Brown retrieved the first man through the surf. The process was repeated until all six were brought to safety. Although all six sailors were now on the beach, exhaustion and hyperthermia set in, and two of their number had to be "restored" to life by their rescuers.

The next maritime casualty was the *Antares*, a "coastal collier" with a shipment of coal destined for Boston.

An example of a Collier

She was a 175-ton vessel with a crew of seven consisting of the captain, mate and five sailors. The *Antares* fell victim to the storm at 9:00 a.m. She washed up just south of the *Arkansas* near the uninhabited marshland north of Goose Pond and adjacent to Logantown.

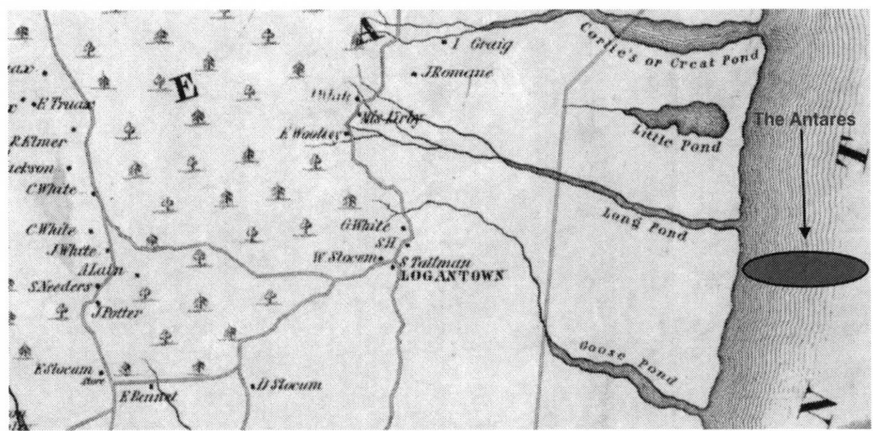

Location of the *Antares*

Similar to the *Arkansas*'s position, she sat head-in to shore, with her stern absorbing the punishment meted out by the surf.

The crew had clambered into the rigging when local resident, William Conroe, discovered her. One of the crew walked across the jib-boom and threw a line to Conroe, who then pulled the crewman to safety. Conroe then successfully cast the line onto the *Antares's* rigging six more times and completed the rescue of the rest of the crew.

The next two wrecks lay close to one another, separated by 300 yards, and their rescues required intervention by the local community.

The first wreck was the ironically named the *New Jersey,* a barque on a return voyage to New York after picking up cotton, hides and iron from Savannah, Georgia. She was situated broadside, eight miles north of Squan (Manasquan Inlet) and twenty-two miles south of Sandy Hook. Like the *Register,* she also carried a single passenger and a crew of twelve, including a cook and steward. Captain Edward Lewis may have been the first to attract the attention of Mr. Garrett Newman, the solitary soul standing on the beach.

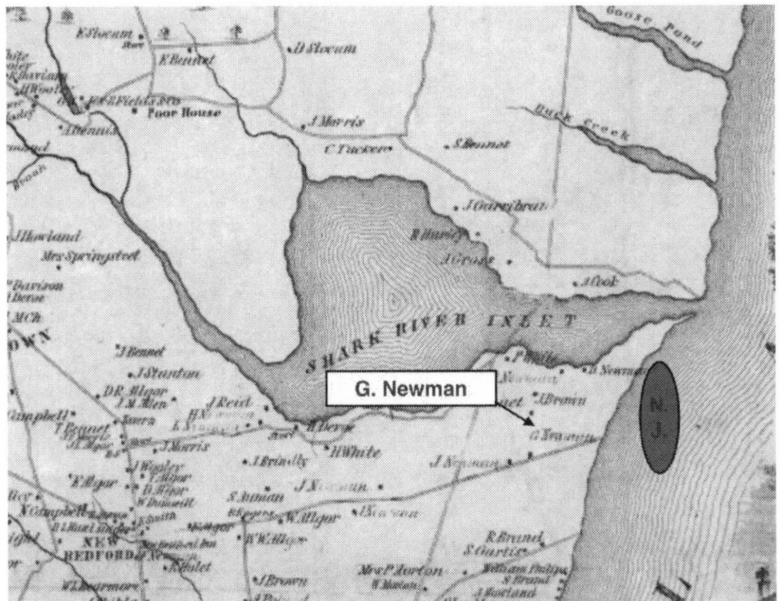

Location of the *New Jersey*

Because of the distance from the shore and the storm's intensity, verbal communication between the two men was impossible. Captain Lewis's crew took the initiative and cast a line towards Newman, standing in ankle-deep water. Despite assistance from wind and tide, the rope never reached Newman after several attempts over the course of the next half hour.

Mutual frustration grew.

Finally, Newman realized if he were to be successful he would need to venture out deeper into the surf. He sensed the raw power of the waves and knew of undertows – both formidable dangers. Alone, he also knew that if he lost his footing it would mean certain death for both himself and the men aboard the *Antares*.

Carefully, he went further out, taking measured steps to ensure his footing was secure. As he went deeper, he directly felt the storm's fury.

Timing his movement to the oncoming waves, he finally secured the rope and retreated to shore. With his extremities numbing, he pulled the rope taut, providing the *New Jersey* crew with a lifeline. The entire crew followed the rope through the breakers and thanked their rescuer.

When all were safely ashore, Newman hustled the men to his home, where a large fire was made to prevent the dangers of frostbite and hypothermia.

Later that morning, other members of the community came to the beach and helped the wreck-master, John Remsen, gather some of the *New Jersey's* cargo for safekeeping. Sometime between 9:00 a.m. and 10:00 a.m., those on the beach noticed a curious sight through the blinding snow and mist. Some thought it was an apparition.

In reality it was a vessel in distress. The ship was heading directly towards them, a few hundred yards at most from where the *New Jersey* lay. This was the *Lotty*.

From the onlookers' perspective, her chances of survival were slim. As one witness recalled, "All saw there was no hope for her".

Because of the ebbing tide, the *Lotty* finally struck bottom further out on a bar, about 300 yards from shore, and through some odd interplay of waves, winds and currents her bow now faced *into* the breakers. Waves now rode up and over her bow, pounding her further into the shoals and stressing the ship's superstructure.

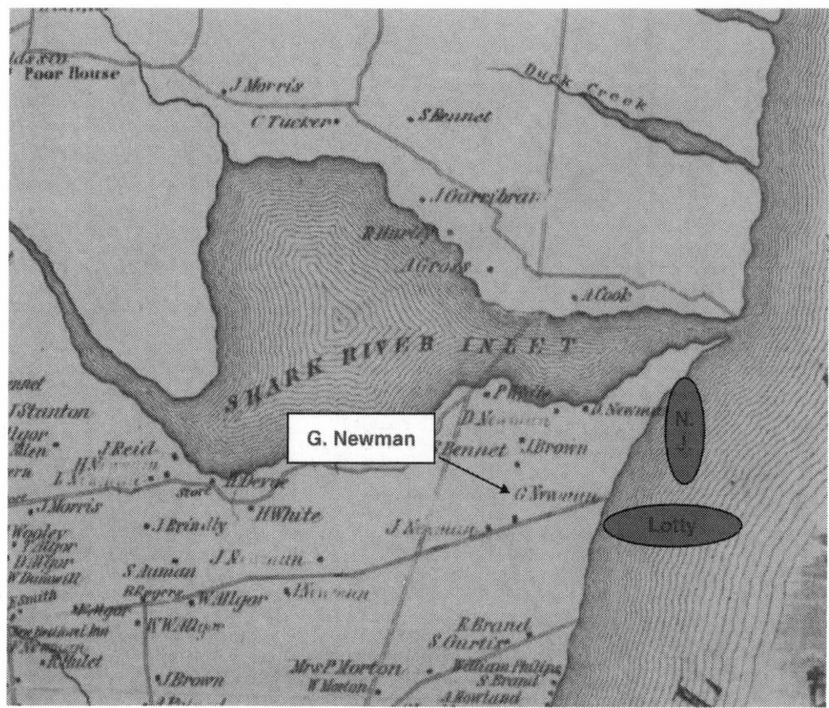

Location of the *New Jersey and Lotty*

Although the vessel was within earshot, an unexpected barrier arose; language. Apparently the ship's crew did not speak English, and those on shore were unfamiliar with the language (it was later learned it was Swedish). Nevertheless, one of the *Lotty's* crewmen decided to effect a rescue on his own by swimming to shore. He was Captain D'Haen, but prior to entering the breakers he fastened documents about his waist. He then walked deliberately to the ship's rear, balanced himself and jumped into the surf.

He appeared to be a "powerful swimmer", and using long, rhythmic strokes he started to make his way towards shore. But despite his apparent abilities, he was unable to gain any headway. Each retreating wave up the beach created a strong riptide, while the storm's currents also pushed him further south.

An eyewitness recorded his struggle:

I also speak of the barque Lotty, as being one of the most heart – rendering scene I ever witnessed. She came ashore within 300 yards of the barque New Jersey, between nine and 10 o'clock, A.M., same day lying head to seaward, the surf making an entire breach over her, and which swept her decks in less than fifteen minutes after she struck. During this time, Captain D'Haen jumped from the tafrail[†] *into the surf, where he was seen struggling for ten or fifteen minutes and then disappeared. It was impossible for any assistance to be rendered from the shore, as there was no boat present, and had there been the sea was such that the people could not have assisted him.*

Meanwhile on the beach, wreckmaster Remsen ordered several men to retrieve the surfboat housed about a mile to the north. But unexpected difficulties lay ahead.

Once the men reached the boathouse, they divided into two groups – one to hitch the horses to the wagon, the other to lift the boat onto the wagon.

As the boat was manhandled onto the wagon, the wind lifted it aloft and it fell onto the sand. Fortunately, it was undamaged. Again it was remounted and this time secured by rope.

However, the horses now refused to budge, either because of the wind's intensity or the intense cold.

---

1. [†] A rail and ornamentation around a ship's stern.

The only remaining option was for the men to drag the boat through the sand. The distance to the wrecks was over one mile.

Back at the beachhead opposite the *Lotty*, two things occupied Remsen's mind: the rescue of Captain D'Haen, and establishing a physical connection to the ship.

D'Haen somehow was able to keep his head above the waves, but he was drifting south very quickly. Several men on shore kept apace of his movements, hoping to pull him to safety when he was close enough. D'Haen often appeared high on a wave, "struggling vainly" for the shore. He was next seen as a "strong swimmer in agony". He finally slipped under the waves and was never seen again.

Further up the beach, the *Lotty* continued to receive a battering from the swells. It culminated in the smashing of her bulkhead, which was swept away. With it went the *Lotty's* mate, who also drowned.

The *Lotty*'s remaining crew tried to save themselves by attaching a rope to a buoy; the goal to have the waves carry it close to shore. However, the conflicting currents foiled all attempts.

Because of the *Lotty's* distance and the onshore winds, Remsen made no attempt to send a line. But a local fisherman had a suggestion. He often fished for squid, and he thought that by adding sufficient lead weight he might be able to cast a line and snag it somewhere aboard the *Lotty*.

Remsen thought it was worth a try. After several attempts, the man snared the biggest catch of his life when the line wrapped itself into the rigging. A slim, fragile line now "communicated" between the shore and the *Lotty.* A rope was attached to this line, and with the help of the *Lotty's* crew, a rope eventually replaced it.

Despite the line connected to the ship, it remained dangerous for anyone from the *Lotty* to make it to shore without assistance. The distance, depth, treacherous surf and the men's clothing all worked against them.

The only way they could be saved was if a surfboat could be launched.

Finally, the surfboat arrived after being hauled across the sand by "30 or 40" men. Remsen asked for volunteers to attempt a rescue. Most of the men thought the notion was pure folly – any volunteer was certain to join the mounting roll of the dead.

To Remsen's astonishment, four men stepped forward: Samuel Brand, William Morton, John Brown and Howland Morton. Wasting no time, Remsen ordered the four into the boat while the rest of the men steadied her. Someone suggested that a rope be fixed to the stern as a precaution.

With one great push, the surfboat was launched head into the breakers while the men aboard pulled on the oars. One of them hung onto the rope connected to the *Lotty* to ensure they were not pulled off course. The *Lotty* sailors could only hope that surfboat would crest each wave and that the rope would remain in place.

As the boat approached the *Lotty,* the line attached to the surfboat's stern ripped away, leaving only the rope connected to the *Lotty* – a connection that represented life and death for the men in the boat and in the *Lotty.* Only through extreme effort did the four men eventually reach the vessel.

The *Lotty* crew quickly dropped into the surfboat. The over-burdened boat now pivoted towards shore – a risky but necessary maneuver – and, using the rope as a guide and riding the incoming surf, all seven men made it to shore.

An eyewitness recorded the rescue:

We returned to the barque Lotty and they're beheld some twelve or more men in the rigging clinging for life and waiting for assistance–time alone could decide their fate, as the surf– boat was a mile off; there were at this time a number of men on the beach, they were sent for the surf– boat, by John Remsen, the wreck-master, and returned in time to save them, although the surf was raging to such a height that it appeared impossible to take them off; but there was some true– hearted and daring men who risked their own lives to save those of the Lotty, and they succeeded in their first attempt. It must be long remembered by the sufferers, as three of their number could not walk when landed upon the beach. They were all taken to the house of Garrett Newman, where their wet clothes were changed and they were made comfortable.

Eight miles south of the *Lotty* and immediately south of the "Squan" inlet lay the schooner *Alabama*. She carried spices and iron from Philadelphia and came ashore at 7:00 a.m., near the home of Thomas Cook.

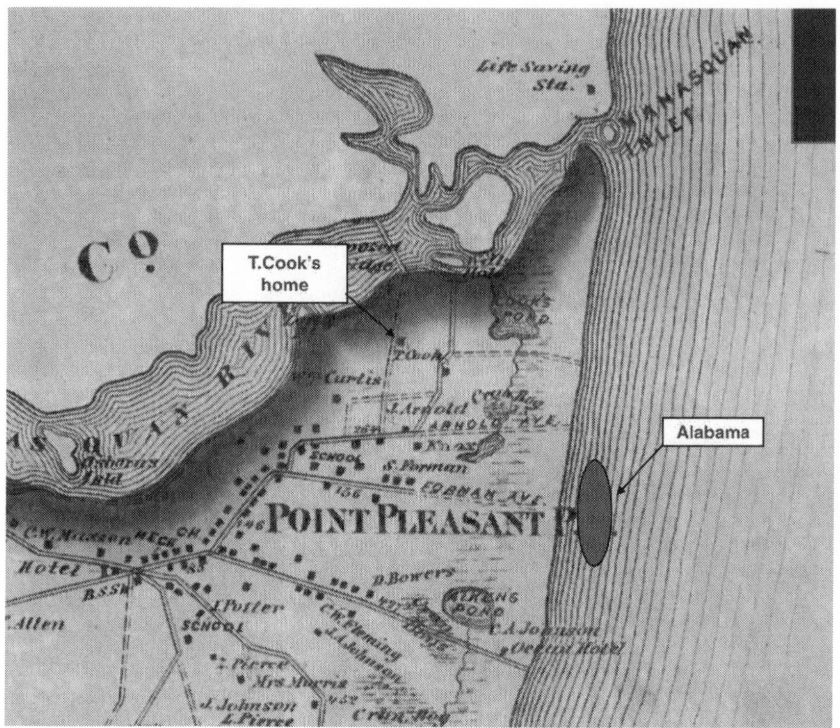

Location of the *Alabama*

Cook found the *Alabama* lying broadside to the shore, rocking in the undertow. Two men hung in the ship's rigging, just a few feet above the deck. It was later learned that the rest of the *Alabama's* crew were already lost.

As the *Alabama* rolled toward the shore, the men in the rigging were submerged in the surf "and almost touched the moving sands of the undertow".

Soon a surfboat from Squan inlet arrived with five men. However, they were forced to turn back because of the heavy surf. It was left to Thomas Cook alone to rescue the two men. He went home for some rope, but when he returned one of the two men was lost in the surf. The vessel soon disintegrated. The only man Cook could retrieve was found to be already dead. Everyone on board the *Alabama* had perished.

The loss of life was a great blow to Point Pleasant's inhabitants. What more could they have done to assist those poor souls? Should the men in the Squan lifeboat have attempted a rescue?

While the inhabitants were lamenting the loss of the *Alabama* crew, they were unaware of the far greater disaster that would unfold over the next 24 hours.

Saturday, February 14th

The *John Minturn* departed New Orleans on January 24, expecting to arrive in New York City in three weeks, sometime around mid-February. A sister ship, the *Orleans,* accompanied her along the East Coast, a custom they had employed in the past.

SHIPPING INTELLIGENCE.

SUNDAY MORNING, JANUARY 25, 1846.

CLEARED YESTERDAY.

Ship Diadem, Barstow, Boston, L H Gale
Ship Serampore, Barker, Boston, F M Weld & Co
Ship Helen, (Br) Hicks, Liverpool, W H Haynes
Ship John Minturn, Stark, New York, J W Stanton & Co
Ship Espindola, Barstow, Liverpool, Jenkins & Tigler
Ship Orleans, Sears, New York, A Cohen
Barque Archimedes, Burkman, New York, C Deake & Co
Barque Rothschild, Lawry, Liberia, (Africa,) G W Hynson
Brig Titi, Brown, Havana, Anguera & Bro
Brig Cadet, Day, Havana, Harrod, Darling & Co
Brig Derigo, Tibbetts, Georgetown, Lindley & Russell
Schr Henry Plantagenet, McNeill, Tampa Bay, Master
Schr Eleun, (Mex) Le Roy, Campeachy, J W Zacharie & Co
Schr Joaquina, Martinez, Sisal, J W Zacharie & Co
Schr Mary Marshall, Johnston, Mobile, H Davis

Departure of the *John Minturn* and the *Orleans* from New Orleans, January 1846 [45]

In the hold of the *Minturn* was a wide range of goods and commodities: hides, pig lead, lard, corn, hams and wheat. The actual inventory was quite extensive:

- 283 bales cotton
- 503 hods and barrels of sugar
- 254 barrels molasses
- 3,000 pig lead
- 100 bales hemp
- 754 bags corn
- 9 tierces and 33 barrels of wax
- 35 barrels wheat
- 5 casks hams
- 106 tierces beef
- 100 casks pork
- 177 barrels lard
- 548 kegs lard
- 42 barrels tallow
- 44 barrels seed
- 13 boxes merchandize
- 16 bales skins
- 947 hides
- 107 bags feathers

- 4 bales, 30 bundles and casks of hair
- 17 barrels and 1 cask of bristles

The cargo’s value was substantial– $80,000 – roughly $2.5 million in today's dollars and the New York merchants of J &A Roberson, S.F. Goodridge, Thomas H. Mayher and Lasala & Company awaited delivery of their goods so they could resell them at a tidy profit.

But the sales prices of their goods were subject to market forces beyond their control. Many of these products – such as cotton, corn, lard, wheat and sugar – were commodity-based and publicly traded, so prices varied according to the law of supply and demand.

For example, a February 5, 1846 New York newspaper column recorded the day's cotton and other commodity prices:

New York, Tuesday night, Feb. 3.—Cotton—There was a better demand for Cotton this morning, and prices were firm. The sales of the last three days amount to 2300 bales, a considerable portion of which was of middling and fair qualities for export. The following are the particulars:—

	Upland and Florida.		Mobile & N. O.	
	1700 bales.		600 bales.	
Inferior............................	none.		none.	
Ordinary to good ordinary.......	6⅛ a 6½	cents	6¼ a 6¾	cents.
Midding to good middling.......	6⅝ a 7⅛	"	7 a 7¾	"
Middling fair to fair.............	7¼ a 7⅝	"	8 a 8½	"
Fully fair to good fair...........	7¾ a 7⅞	"	8¾ a 9¼	"
Fine..............................	nom.		nom.	

Flour is steady at $5 53 @ 5 62½ for Michigan, Ohio and Genesee. 2500 bbls Genesee were taken at 5 62½, and 1000 do Michigan, &c., a mixed lot, at 5 56¼. Southern flour is dull—Baltimore Howard st. and City Mills 5 37½ @ 5 50—Georgetown 5 50 @ 5 62½—Alexandria, Petersburg, &c, 5 37½ @ 5 50. Rye flour $4 @ 4 25—Corm Meal $4 @ 4 12½ in barrels and 17 50 in hhds. 2600 bus southern old Corn of good quality sold at 64c, and 2600 do new do at the same price. Ashes—100 bbls Pots sold at 3 87½ @ $4, the latter price for this year's brand—40 bbls Pearls sold at 4 25. Provisions are inactive—Mess Pork at $11 75 @ 13 25—prime do 9 75 @ 10 50—Beef $8 @ 8 50 and 5 25 @ 5 50 for mess and prime. Butter is in fair demand at 14 @ 20c, according to quality—Lard 7¾ @ 8½c—Cheese 7 @ 7½c in casks and boxes. Whiskey is inactive at 23 @ 24c in drudge casks and barrels. Sugars are steady—200 hhds New Orleans and New Iberia sold within the last three [46]

New York Quoted Cotton prices from February 5, 1846

According to this excerpt, cotton sourced from Mobile (Alabama) and N.O. (New Orleans) commanded a premium over cotton shipped from other U.S. ports (left column). That made the price of the *Minturn's* 283 bales particularly valuable in February, if prices held up and the cotton was delivered undamaged.

Typically, the delivery of goods was accompanied by a Bill of Lading, a memorandum signed by the ship's master acknowledging the receipt of goods, and a promise to deliver them in the same condition as received. For each of the goods listed aboard the *Minturn,* Captain Stark would have signed a document similar to the following:

[Sold by H. Cowperthwait, Front st. Philadelphia.]

SHIPPED,

In good order, and well conditioned, by Thomas Martin *in and upon the good* Schr *called the* Henry Clay *whereof is Master for this present Voyage,* Ahira Hall *now lying in the port of Philadelphia, and bound for* Providence *To say,*

Thirty five Barrels Starch

Being marked and numbered as in the margin, and are to be delivered in the like good Order, and condition, at the port of Providence *(the dangers of the Seas only excepted,) unto* Horace Borden *or to* his *Assigns, he or they paying freight for the said Goods,*

Twenty five Cents per Barrel

with Primage and Average accustomed. In witness whereof, the Master or Purser of the said Schr *hath affirmed to* three *Bills of Lading, all of this Tenor and Date; one of which being accomplished, the others to stand void. Dated Philadelphia, the* twenty eighth *day of* ~~November~~ 1829

Ahira Hall

Philad^a 10th Month 18th 1829

Thomas Martin

Bought of Blackstone Mfg Co

Thirty five Barrels Starch viz

Gross	Tare	Gross	Tare	Gross	Tare	Gross	Tare	Gross	Tare
175	16	180	18	190	18	190	18	179	18
184	18	182	18	182	16	184	18	178	18
188	18	180	18	179	16	182	18	180	18
183	18	188	17	176	16	175	18	178	18
182	18	177	18	181	18	177	18	176	18
179	18	187	18	181	18	175	17	202	19
189	18	183	18	176	16	183	18	173	17

Weighing Gross 6346 lbs
Tare 619 Nett 5727 lbs @ 6¢ $ 343.62
Barrels 20¢ each 7.00
Porterage 1.50
$ 352.12

Cash

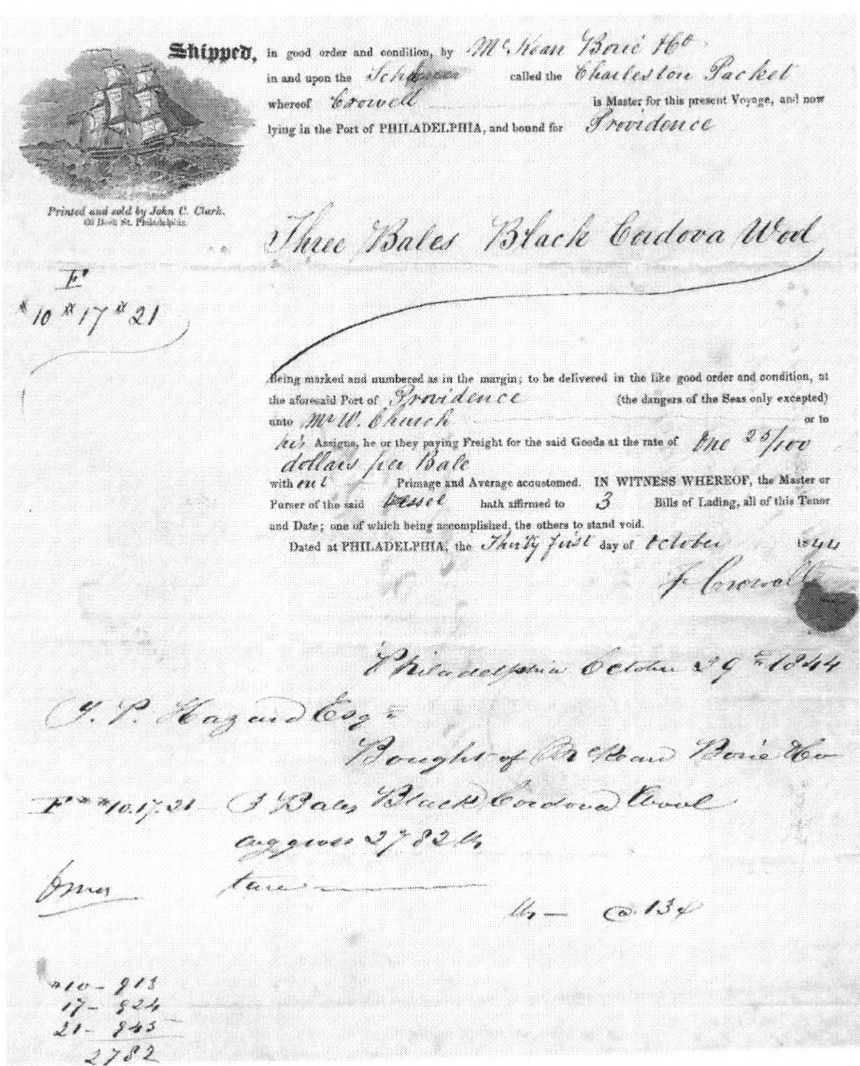

Shipped, in good order and condition, by McKean Borie & Co in and upon the Schooner called the Charleston Packet whereof Crowell is Master for this present Voyage, and now lying in the Port of PHILADELPHIA, and bound for Providence

Printed and sold by John C. Clark, [illegible] Dock St. Philadelphia.

Three Bales Black Cordova Wool

F
10 17 21

Being marked and numbered as in the margin; to be delivered in the like good order and condition, at the aforesaid Port of Providence (the dangers of the Seas only excepted) unto Mr W. Church or to his Assigns, he or they paying Freight for the said Goods at the rate of one 25/100 dollars per Bale with out Primage and Average accustomed. IN WITNESS WHEREOF, the Master or Purser of the said Vessel hath affirmed to 3 Bills of Lading, all of this Tenor and Date; one of which being accomplished, the others to stand void.

Dated at PHILADELPHIA, the Thirty first day of October 1844

F Crowell

Philadelphia October 29 1844

[illegible] Hazard Esq

Bought of McKean Borie & Co

F 10.17.21 3 Bales Black Cordova Wool

aggross 2782 lb

tare

lb @ 13¢

10 - 913
17 - 924
21 - 945
2782

Two examples of Bills of Lading –
(Previous) 1829 transport of thirty-five barrels of starch aboard the ship *Henry Clay* from Philadelphia to Providence.
(Above) 1844 transport of three bales of Black Cordova Wool aboard the schooner *Charleston Packet* from Philadelphia to Providence. (From the author's collection)

On this winter's run the *Minturn* was not just a cargo ship; she also carried twenty-nine passengers. There was a handful of civilians – a printer, a butcher and a newlywed couple – but the majority of the passengers were able-bodied seamen. These were the survivors of the *Van Buren* and *Cherokee* disasters, both vessels recently lost off the southern coast.

For these twenty-two sailors, the trip north was to be a leisurely experience; no need to furl and unfurl sails, climb into the rigging or stand late night watches. During this journey they were "mere" passengers. The sailing responsibilities were left to the *Minturn*'s commander and his own twenty-odd crewmembers.

For the *Minturn*, the seamen passengers also served as a kind of insurance policy; they were individual reserves that could be called into action in an emergency, perhaps due to the illness or injury of a *Minturn* crewmen, but nothing more. Having this second contingent aboard provided an added measure of comfort to both the civilian passengers and Captain Stark alike.

But given the ship's steady progress and the favorable weather conditions, the need to employ these resources seemed highly unlikely. So far, the journey from the Florida Keys to the southern coast of New Jersey had been uneventful.

For fifty-one year-old Captain Dudley Stark, completing this voyage had far greater meaning than just the mere transfer of some barrels of molasses, kegs of lard and some hard-luck sailors.

He had two great personal stakes in its success.

Foremost in his mind was the safe transport of his family to their home in Stonington, Connecticut. Aboard were his wife Catherine, their fifteen year-old son Stephen and twelve-year-old daughter Helen. This indeed was Stark's most precious cargo.

Why the family was returning to Connecticut in February is unknown. But something dark was troubling Stark. It was something he could escape from when at sea and something he may have hidden even from his wife, Catherine.

The fact was Captain Dudley Stark was insolvent.

Over the years, he had amassed a number of outstanding debts, some as small as 84 cents and others as large as a thousand dollars. Some debts were attached to interest-bearing promissory notes; others appeared to be casual verbal promises of repayment. And although many of the individual amounts were not large, Captain Dudley Stark had many, many creditors.

Perhaps relieving the stress of his pressing debts played a role in undertaking a risky winter run up to New York. But one thing was apparent; he needed to retire these debts soon and he hoped to make a number of profitable runs in 1846. Perhaps the success of this February trip would be an omen of more profitable things to come.

But first he needed to deliver his passengers and goods to New York. They were almost there.

Late Friday, February 13, the *Minturn* made progress north and was comfortably astride the New Jersey coastline. For the superstitious aboard, the thirteenth day of the month was passing uneventfully and a waning moon illuminated the crisp clear skies.

The following morning, Saturday, presented another welcoming sea and sky, with the ship located only about thirty miles south of Atlantic Highlands and approximately forty-five miles from her slip in New York Harbor.

Her location, speed and the present sea conditions suggested the *Minturn* would arrive in lower Manhattan sometime early on Sunday morning, in time for the more devoted to attend services at Broadway's Trinity Church.

In *America's Victory: The Heroic Story of a Team of Ordinary Americans And How They Won the Greatest Yacht Race Ever,* David Shaw explains in detail the events on board the *John Minturn* that Saturday. The author first describes the circumstances regarding the pilot boat *Blossom*'s initial attempt to work with the *John Minturn*:

The pilots cursed quietly. Bad weather was right over the horizon. The men knew the signs well. Sailing slowly, however, their schooner stood less of a chance to chase down some of the many ships bound for New York, put aboard the remaining pilots, and run for port before the storm hit. A large blue flag indicating that pilots were still available and ready to work flew from a tender pole at the truck of the main topmast...

Not far from the Blossom were at least half a dozen ships heading north toward New York Harbor. The schooners Pioneer, Alabama, and Register, the bark New Jersey, and the fully rigged sailing packets Orleans and John Minturn ghosted along with the wind fair astern. Most of these ships had already taken on a pilot but several of the ships, including the Orleans and John Minturn, still required a pilot. At approximately nine o'clock (a.m.), Blossom sighted the brig Moses and dispatched a pilot, leaving two [pilots] aboard. Shortly thereafter, two other ships hove into view. Slowly, Blossom sailed up to the nearest vessel [the John Minturn] and sent pilot Thomas Freeborne(sic) to board her.

Standing on the poop deck of the packet John Minturn, Captain Starke (sic) watched with indifference as the nearby pilot boat lowered her yawl...the flags [on the schooner] indicated [to Stark] that the schooner was one of the New York boats.

"Keep her sails full and drawing" Starke said to his first officer. "Perhaps the man will see he's not wanted here."

In such faint winds, the oarsmen in the yawl had no trouble catching up to the ship. As the yawl pulled close to the vessel, Thomas Freeborne (sic) noted that there was no ladder hung over the ship's side to allow him to climb aboard. He sighed. Craning his neck, he peered up at the officers on deck. "This is Thomas Freeborne of the pilot boat Blossom. I'll come aboard, Captain!"

Stark strode to the rail and gazed down at Freeborne. "Off with ye now!" he yelled. "I'll not take a man from a New York boat."

"As you wish, Captain. Put her about, lads," he said to the apprentices at the oars of the yawl. The boys glumly struck out for the row back to the schooner...[47]

After Stark's rude dismissal of Freeborn, the *Blossom* continued to search for other vessels in need of pilots. As the day progressed and more pilots took engagements, the ranks of the pilots aboard the *Blossom* grew smaller.

Throughout the day the Blossom cruised up and down the coast looking for inbound ships, and throughout the day the weather deteriorated. The southwesterly winds increased, suddenly shifted to the northeast, and came in strong. Waves formed atop the swells, gradually began to break. The temperature plummeted to below freezing and it began to snow.[48]

Aboard the *Minturn*, several hours passed and she was still without a Sandy Hook pilot. As night drew closer, the *Blossom* once again approached the *John Minturn*:

At around five o'clock, Blossom again caught sight of the John Minturn and this time she signaled for a pilot.

This was a full eight hours after her first engagement with the *Minturn*. Stark's initial bias had caused an unwarranted delay which would later prove deadly.

Thomas Freeborne (sic) gripped the rails of the yawl as the apprentices worked hard at the oars, their muscles bulging unseen under the oilskins with every stroke. The bow of the little rowboat plunged deep into the breaking crests. Spray and snow soaked Freeborne's face, his southwester pulled low over his head, partially obscuring his weathered cheeks. His silk top hat he had left behind aboard the schooner. However, he still wore his heavy frock coat and a knit wool sweater underneath it to keep warm. John Minturn's hull towered above him. His boatmen drew close alongside. Timing the rise and fall of the yawl with the rhythm of the sea, he stood up in the boat as it rose to the top of a large wave, and grabbed the rope ladder hung over the side of the ship. In less than a minute, Freeborne was aboard.

Captain Starke clasped Freeborne's hand and apologized for waving him off earlier that day.

"I understand. There are many of us who wish things were different," Freeborn replied, turning his back against the wind to peer westward through the whirling snow. He estimated the dangers of the beach lay just four miles away. "We've got to get her offshore!" Freeborne shouted.[49]

Freeborn's arrival was confirmation to both passengers and crew that their journey was nearing an end. Here was a New York Harbor pilot helping them navigate through the "Narrows" and up the Hudson River and onto an awaiting slip.

Stark and Freeborn walked towards the captain's cabin to discuss their final approach into the harbor. Even while the two men were conversing, the conditions had deteriorated further. The sky had darkened considerably, ushering in an early start to nightfall, but it was the change in the wind that was most noticeable. It now blew steadily from the north and east, a very bad sign for those familiar with the most feared of Atlantic winter storms, the Nor'easter.

An hour later – at 6:00 p.m. – the steering sails were taken in and the ship was now hauled to the wind. As the wind increased, Freeborn ordered the topgallant sail and topsails single reefed[‡].

Freeborn next ordered the double-reefing of the topsails, the process used to reduce the sail's exposure even further.

According to one crewman, "[Stark] did not think the sails needed double reefing," thus overruling Freeborn's request. Perhaps this was more evidence of Stark's prejudice of New York pilots. For now, the sails remained as they were, single-reefed.

[‡] Reefing was used to reduce a sail's area, an operation used especially when the wind speed increased and the ship no longer needed a large surface area of sail.

At 7:00 p.m., the *Minturn* was forced to turn under a north north-east heading, steering directly into the teeth of the storm. Just two hours later, at 9:00 p.m. the wind increased to gale force.

Freeborn again recommended the topsails be double-reefed, the mainsail hauled up, reefed and furled. Speed was not the issue for the *Minturn*, control, however was vital. This time when Freeborn urged a reduction in sail, Stark reluctantly yielded.

Perhaps another reason for Stark's hesitancy for reducing sail had more to do with his knowledge of the ship's poor condition, rather than seamanship. As the foresail was hauled up, it "blew to pieces", according to one account, taking with it the jib and the spanker. The cause was obvious to the crew: all the running gear was rotten.

The *Minturn,* with the loss of sails, had sustained its first foray with the storm. In addition to the fierce winds and frigid temperatures, blinding snow was another factor she needed to face.

Any thought that the storm would soon exhaust itself or pass out to sea was soon dismissed. If anything its intensity increased. However, the Captain comforted himself that they were close to the harbor and would soon realize the protection of a deep-water port.

As midnight came and the storm was still gathering strength, the wind was howling at fifty to sixty miles per hour from the north and east.
All hands were pressed into service, most likely joined by the crewmen from the *Van Buren* and *Cherokee.* All on board now shared a growing state of urgency.

Freeborn again ordered a further shortening of sail: this time, the topsails were to be close-reefed. However, he received a stern warning – not from Stark – but from the *Minturn's* first and second mate:

If anything was started about the topsails, they would blow to pieces, they being so old and worn out.

Confirming their prediction, the main and mizen topsails did indeed blow away, followed quickly by the foretopsail. The *Minturn* was slowly being de-masted, losing her ability to control her course. She now fell off before the wind.

Freeborn next ordered all fore, aft and mainsail top sails reefed.

According to one crew member:

After the topsails blew away, the forelifts parted, and the foreyard, having the foresail hauled up to it, canted a cockbill, so we had to lash the larboard yardarm to the rail, which rendered the foresail useless.

The battle with the storm continued through the night and into the early morning, meanwhile more spars and tackle were destroyed. The crew fought to keep the ship off the coast.

The consensus opinion was to survive until daylight. Surely the storm's severity would soon abate.

Sunday, February 15th

When morning finally arrived, the *Minturn* was in a compromised state. She was now ill-equipped to navigate in a storm as severe as this. Her crew was exhausted, having worked throughout the night despite relief help from the sailors of the *Cherokee* and *Van Buren.* The ship's equipment was in a worse state, her sails either lost or shredded.

But most dispiriting, the storm of the previous day continued in ferocity, seemingly bent on destroying the *John Minturn.*

At 7:00 a.m. the ship now encountered blizzard conditions. Without fore and aft sails the *Minturn* was at the mercy of the northern and easterly currents pushing her ever closer to the New Jersey shore.

Freeborn still hoped to acquire some control and asked for any spare sails. "None but an old maintopsail," came the response. Freeborn decided not to employ it.

The tempestuous weather in the meantime had increased considerably. Every sail [of the Minturn] was torn almost to ribbons by the violence of the wind, and the ship rendered unmanageable.

His next decision was something uncharacteristic in maritime leadership; he called the ship's officers, passengers and the more experienced crew to a meeting to decide on a course of action. He shared with them his professional assessment; they were drifting inexorably towards the coast and the ship would ultimately be lost and tossed into the breakers. But if they followed his suggestion, some lives might be spared.

His recommendation; put the ship's head before the wind and run the vessel over the shoals and as close to the beach as possible. There, with assistance from the any inhabitants they would stand the best chance of rescue.

Whether Captain Stark endorsed the plan or not is unknown. Stark's first concern, of course, would have been the safety of his immediate family, his passengers and crew, in that order.

But privately he must have had reservations. This plan meant the total loss of the *Minturn* (of which he was a part-owner) and the disastrous consequences to his personal finances.

And the plan assumed not just sacrificing the ship, but the loss of all cargo. The bales of cotton and hemp, the barrels of sugar and wheat, the casks of hams and pork would all be lost. Any compensation he could have earned would have reduced his mounting financial losses.

Furthermore, he would need to explain to his business partners why he was unable to avoid the disaster. Had he kept the ship properly maintained? Should he have kept it further out to sea? Should he have accepted the first offer from the New York pilot boat? Could he somehow have avoided the storm? Was there adequate insurance to cover their losses? The cargo? What about the wages he would owe to the crew?

Moreover, with the loss of the *Minturn*, he would also be without a source of income, further escalating his indebtedness. These concerns would have caused anxiety as he sought desperately to avoid beaching his ship on the shoals.

The wind continued at gale force, and for the next two hours the storm's strong currents were controlling the *Minturn's* direction. The only questions remaining were; where and when would the *Minturn* strike the beach.

At 9:00 a.m. Freeborn instructed the crew to double-reef the top sails and furl the mainsail.

As the mainsail was being hauled in, it blew completely away from the ship owing to "the running gear [being] rotten."

1846 Currier and Ives lithograph of the *John Minturn*

Suddenly, land came dimly into view, but most alarmingly, the thunderous crescendo of breakers could be heard above the wind. The sound brought on a state of panic. The moment that would determine one's survival had arrived.

Freeborn maintained his composure as he carefully steered the ship as best he could over the first set of shoals, informing all to prepare for a bumpy ride and a sudden arrest.

The tattered mainsail was then hauled in and the yards squared parallel to the shore. The *Minturn* caught an incoming swell like a modern-day surfer, riding it towards shore until the next swell overtook it. The ship's speed picked up while everyone aboard braced themselves. The time was now 9:30 a.m.

The *John Minturn* thumped hard against the outer bar, 300 yards from the beach. However, she held that position only momentarily. Another swell passed under the hull, lifting her stern and carrying her another 100 yards. This should have been a favorable result, except the ship no longer had her weight supported by the ocean and "broke her back". She split in two, although not entirely. Freeborn ordered the masts cut away, hoping to keep the two halves from further disintegration. "She continued to thump and grind terribly":

The horror and confusion at the moment of her striking were terrific, and when the worst was known, every effort was made to preserve the lives of those on board.

The first witnesses to the *Minturn*'s struggle were George Johnson, James Dorset and John Van Note. The men had previously assisted at the *Alabama* wreck when they observed the *Minturn* passing far to the south.

The three chased the *Minturn* along a parallel course, but the vessel moved so rapidly they did not actually see her come ashore, some three and half miles away.

As they worked their way south, flooding across the peninsula slowed their progress. The storm had cut many furrows through the beach, forming temporary "glades" two to five feet deep. In several places the ocean had broached clear across the narrow peninsula, the waters merging into the bay.

When Johnson, Dorset and Van Note finally arrived at the wreck site, the *John Minturn* rested just two hundred yards into the surf. It was located just south of James Herbert's shanty, the only habitation between that location and the head of the bay.

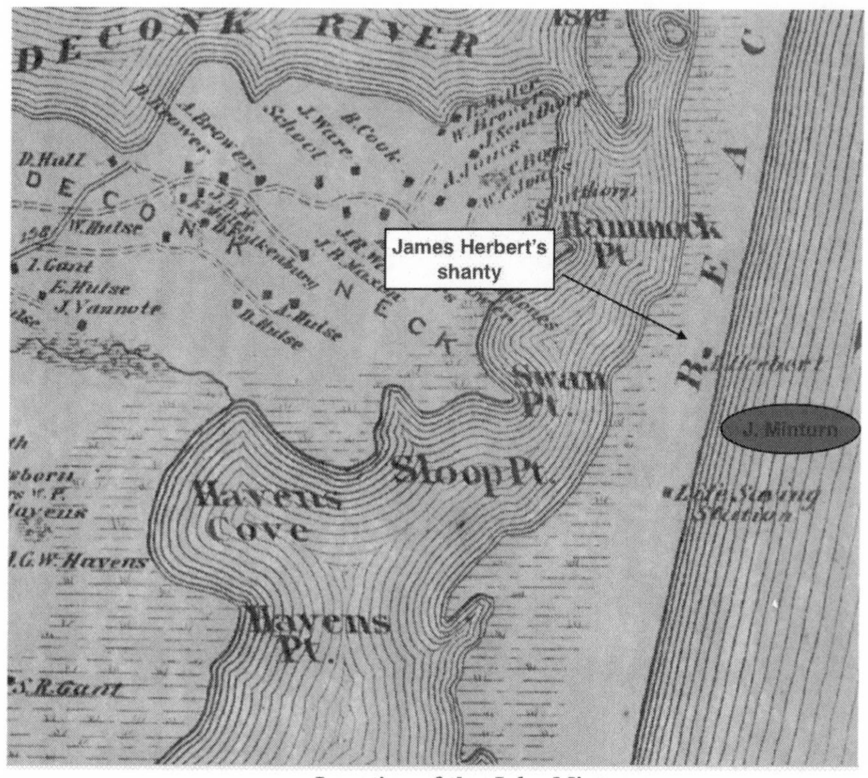

Location of the *John Minturn*

According to one witness:

The most fearful storm I had ever witnessed was that of February 14, 1846. I was awakened at four o'clock in the morning, by the shaking of my bed, as the wind threatened to blow the house from its foundations. While the storm was at its height, about nine o'clock in the morning, we saw just off the shore, through the spray and sleet, the John Minturn, an American barque, with all her sails swept away, drifting to the southward, and approaching shore. She struck to the south of us, about an hour later...

Soon would-be rescuers arrived.

With the surf continuously pounding the ship, Stark decided to send one of his boats ashore. However, as the boat was lowered it "stove in" and joined the spars tossed about in the waves. Stark then ordered a longboat to be launched, with a rope attached to its stern. Six men, five crewmembers and a Portuguese passenger entered the craft.

The longboat soon cleared the *Minturn,* but the strong currents carried it south, parallel to the beach. The rope, which was still attached to the *Minturn,* grew taut. The boat was now in danger of capsizing:

They could not pay out from aboard (the Minturn), as the boat was in the undertow, in the surf, they had to cut the line to save their lives. The loss of rope was truly disastrous...

An experienced surfman on the shore, John Maxon, saw that they must founder, and cried "cut the line!" An instant hesitation would have cost them their lives ...The [longboat's] crew parted it and the boat was carried by the current to the south. People on shore followed it and as it approached land they "formed a rope of hands" – one on their ends resting on the shore, the others pushed into the sea, into the very power of the undertow, and as waves were curling over it, seized the boat and brought it to shore.

Although the longboat was now ashore, unfortunately its design was useless to deploy against the heavy incoming surf. There it would sit for the duration of the coming ordeal.

At ten o'clock there were many big boned Jersey-men on the beach, and all on board [the Minturn] had good hopes. The pilot, Freeborn, who thought the men on shore were human, cheered all hands by his encouraging voice and manner.

Freeborn, cold and thoroughly soaked by the waves, knew first-hand the effects of cold and hypothermia. As a nineteen-year-old apprentice he had assisted a man to shore, when the passenger was accidently staved in by their boat. The yawl quickly sunk, and Freeborn and a fellow apprentice spent the next several hours clinging to an oar. Although Freeborn offered encouragement, after a while his peer said, "I am going, Tom, God bless you," and slipped under the waves. Despite the harsh conditions, Freeborn was able to survive the ordeal.

Freeborn understood a major factor to survival was a positive attitude, something he was conveying to everyone aboard the *Minturn*.

The six *Minturn* survivors remained huddled on the beach, hoping they would soon be joined with their fellow passengers and crew. However, the blizzard forced them to move to a nearby shelter:

Being exposed to the full violence of the sea, and a piercing cold wind, ice soon formed over the surface of their drenched clothing. In this state they remained until noon...

To the disbelief of those aboard the *Minturn,* no rescue attempts were made over the next several hours:

Towards noon, all on board who were alive, for some had already sunk under their terrible sufferings, went forward to the top gallant forecastle, where they lashed themselves as best [they] could, to prevent the sea from washing them off. Captain Stark and his mate, together with the pilot remained, it is thought, in the poop cabin.

When noon arrived, there were still no plans for a rescue boat. There were feeble attempts by those on shore to send barrels and ropes out to the *Minturn,* but the conflicting currents thwarted each effort.

And where was the wreck master?

Wreckmaster Hugh Johnson was attending to the *Alabama* calamity some three and half miles to the north. He and his men were recovering bodies, collecting cargo and coordinating activities. Johnson himself was soaked through and trying to stave off hypothermia.

Word of the developing *Minturn* situation did not reach him until around 1:00 p.m. When he realized he was facing a formidable disaster he ordered his crew to bring the surfboat to the scene. However, several factors would inhibit their efforts:

- His men were scattered miles along the shoreline;
- The surfboat was another mile north of the *Alabama,* four and a half miles from the *Minturn;* and
- The boat needed to be transported by men over several breaches on the peninsula; the same path taken earlier by George Johnson, Dorset and Van Note.

And there was a question about Johnson's abilities as a wreck-master. In the words of one official:

Unfortunately, the former efficient wreck master, John S. Foreman, was removed from office on account of his politics, and a man with little skill, and less energy, has his place.

Several hours passed before Johnson arrived at the beachhead opposite the *Minturn.*

The *Minturn* was in its death throes, having received no assistance from the shore and none apparently forthcoming. The fact was later noted:

All this time the vessel was so near the shore that had any effort whatever been made, by procuring a boat, every soul on board might have been saved.

Aboard the *Minturn,* passengers and crew were seeking shelter from the surf:

Pilot Freeborn now gave his greatcoat to [Captain] Stark's wife and children and they gladly huddled inside, bracing themselves against the icy winds and serious wave action.

The top-gallant forecastle was crowded with the passengers and crew, among them Mrs. Stark, with her son, a fine manly boy of

12 or 14 years of age, who had behaved throughout with a coolness and courage far beyond his years, her daughter, the female servant and Mrs. Forbes, the wife of Mr. Forbes, one of the cabin passengers. In the early part of the day, Mrs. Stark was thrown down by a water cask, which had broken adrift, and one side of her face was entirely laid open, but she uttered no murmurs or complaints, seeming anxious only for the safety of her husband and beloved children.

Hour after hour passed – some of the sufferers, stout men, dying from time to time – but still there was no succor, and yet Freeborn was on the alert, active in the cause of humanity, sheltering with his own clothes and all he could gather, the women and children.

As dusk approached, the *Minturn*'s state worsened:

In the afternoon the forecastle broke in two, fore and aft, and about half of those lashed to it were precipitated into the wreck beneath, where they met an instantaneous death.

Fifteen of the unhappy sufferers, including the captain's wife and children and a female steerage passenger, with an infant, were clustered around the stump of the foremast, exposed for nearly twelve hours to all the fury of the storm, and ten of these died there before any attempt was made to rescue them. Mrs Stark, about five minutes before she breathed her last, turned to King, the sailor, and begged him to save her husband and children, but they had all gone before her.

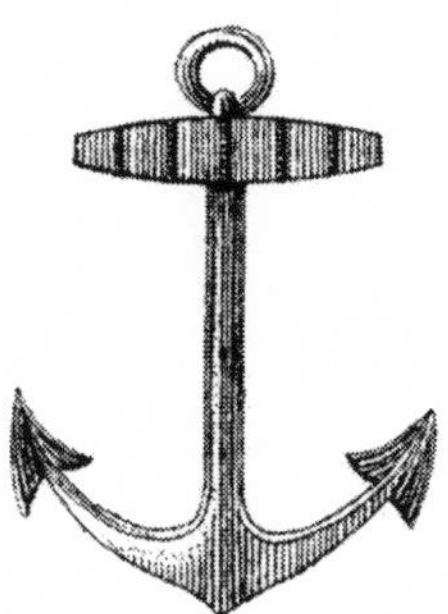

The surfboat finally arrived late that afternoon or early evening. But its presence did not immediately change the rescue operations. The dangers of the surf were magnified because spars, rigging and barrels were frequently launched about in the waves.

To entice volunteers to launch the surfboat, Johnson offered ten, then twenty dollars to any man who would assist. No one volunteered.

They refused the money, and said "We will go off without money as soon as with."

WRECK OF THE JOHN MINTURN.
50

Some from the *Minturn* did reach the shore on their own, but not always with good results:

The female steerage passenger, who had an infant at the breast, died in Mr King's arms.

Complete darkness descended about 12 hours after the *Minturn* first came ashore. She then succumbed to the storm that would later be synonymous with her name.

The tide rose, and the ship broke up rapidly. The top-gallant forecastle collapsed pitching Captain Stark, with Freeborn, all fell into the forward part of the ship; the broken timbers were tossed about for a moment, and the shrieks of the dying ceased. Some of these on other parts of the broken ship were washed ashore with life. Thus perished Thomas Freeborn and with him thirty-seven others.

When the surf was manageable hours later, the surfboat was launched to rescue some survivors still in the breakers.

Between 10 and 11 at night a boat came from the shore, and took off the survivors, viz: the second mate, two of the crew and four of the steerage passengers, who lived through the awful scene, making thirteen saved out of fifty-one.

One rescuer was Joseph Borden, who later gave this account:

We took off six persons, part by boat and part by lines. I threw the line to one man to make it fast around him, but he made it fast to the wreck. He appeared to be pretty much gone, but helped himself along by the rope as well as he could when a sea struck him and threw him clear of the wreck, but he held onto the rope with one hand. I ran down further into the surf and took hold of him; he was all under the water except for one hand and arm. He caught me by the thigh under water, tearing my pantaloons with his other hand. With the help of another surfman, (we) managed to drag the man ashore.

Borden was assisted by Lewis Johnson, Taber Sherman, Elias Allen, Thomas Sculthorpe, Samuel Sherman and John Maxon. They worked for hours to retrieve survivors via lines.

The last to be rescued was John Sturgis, the second mate, who was so stiff from the cold he could barely help himself. After we got all the living men I went to the shanty, the rescued men were all there, and one man was insensible, yet still alive. He seemed to have spasms; they tried to get a little warm drink down him but his teeth were so set they could not. He died in about a quarter hour in great agony.

Aftermath

Although the greatest loss of life occurred off the New Jersey coast, the storm also caused havoc up the entire east coast.

In a letter dated February 16 from Charleston, a ship's captain related his experience from the "Minturn storm":

I arrived this day [Feb. 16] after a long and very rough passage of 55 days, had some very heavy gales of wind carried away main yard, four topsail yards & jib boom and split sails…

Letter written by Charleston's ship captain, dated February 16, 1846

There were many newspaper reports noting the storm's severity:

At New London, Conn, the storm was very severe. The snow in some places was five and six feet deep and at Boston ten feet in drifts. The Transcript of Monday says:

We do not remember such a storm for many years. The drifts in many places were to the height of ten feet...The railroad tracks are of course all blocked up, and a good deal of labor will be required to free them from their heavy encumbrance – Extra engines, with snow ploughs, and large gangs of men, have been sent out upon all the roads. The Boston papers record several marine disasters. The New London, Conn. papers notice the loss of several vessels and life, a printer named Cunningham having been drowned.[51]

The Long Island Train will leave as usual this morning for Boston, at 7 o'clock. The snow has been removed from off the track, which was found to be more encumbered from Riverhead to Greenport, than this side...the snow drifted in some places as high as 15 to 20 feet in the neighborhood of Riverhead...[52]

Initial newspaper reports also counted the *Orleans* – the ship accompanying the *John Minturn* north from New Orleans – as another maritime victim. According to the article the *Orleans* was "completely wrecked." [53]

The ship Orleans, Captain Sears, from New Orleans for New York, was also driven ashore near the same place [as the Minturn], and several of her crew are supposed to have perished.[54]

A few days later, the record was corrected:

It turns out that the packet-ship Orleans was not lost. Today she was towed up to the city by a tow-boat in safety.[55]

Although the *Orleans* and the *Minturn* were close to one another on Saturday, February 14, the *Orleans* somehow avoided disaster and reached New York Harbor. This fact begged the question; why hadn't the *John Minturn* accompanied her?

As for the ship that once was the *Minturn*, little of the vessel was recognizable:

The ship has gone to pieces, nothing remaining of her except the bottom, which is embedded in the sand by the weight of the pig lead which formed part of the cargo. One of the sides and stern and bow have drifted away, and are lying about a mile apart from each other. [56]

The trail of wreckage – both human and cargo – gradually washed ashore and the grim task of collecting, processing and identifying bodies had begun.

When the day broke again [Monday, February, 16] we saw the bow of the boat still remained intact and a group still huddled together upon it. One mother could be seen, with her babe clasped to her breast, her hair streaming in the wind, and her white face turned upward in prayer, appealing to Him who ruled above the war of the elements. When this section broke up, it was found that every one of the group had been dead for many hours.

In the wreck of the forecastle, 16 bodies were found lying in a cluster round the stump of the foremast, and it seemed as if the unfortunate creatures had huddled themselves together for warmth. Among them could be recognized the captain's wife, his children, and a female steerage passenger with an infant at her breast , and so firmly grasped that they could not be separated and they were thus buried.[57]

Forty-one bodies have been found up to Thursday morning, 11 buried, 22 remaining in the church, and eight in the dead house. The body of Capt. Stark was horribly mangled. His shoulder blade was broken and both his legs, showing how desperate were his efforts to save his family and those around him. The bodies of his wife, son, daughter and servant have all been recovered. Many of the bodies remained unclaimed by their friends, and some are unknown.[58]

There were on board, fifty-one persons, all told. Thirteen having been saved, among whom we are glad to find the second mate, Mr. Sturgis, who was last reported lost. Thirty one bodies from her have been recovered, and among them are the wife and two children of Captain Stark, Mr and Mrs Kuhler, and some others of the passengers, whose names are not known.[59]

Mournful Sight – On Saturday the bodies of the unfortunate passengers and sailors who were drowned by the wreck of the Minturn, were brought to the "West Turnout", on the Camden and Amboy Railroad, to await the cars for New York. There were three sled loads of them, and their friends, who had collected to accompany them from Squam Beach, were there with them. It was truly a melancholy sight...[60]

Some of the bodies were later discovered five to seven miles from the site of the wreck.

However one of the bodies not found was widely reported. The search for Thomas Freeborn remained the highest priority for the members of the New York Pilots association:

The body of Captain Thomas Freeborn, the New York pilot, has not been found yesterday morning. His brother is on the beach searching for him.[61]

No loss, since that of the New York pilot boat Gratitude, has caused such a general and paralyzing grief among the pilots and their friends, as that of this inestimable, zealous and fearless man, who was dearly devoted by an extensive circle of acquaintance. The sorrow of his mother and sister is not to be assuaged. Many mourn him as a brother, for the angry waves never engulfed a nobler sailor.

From the seamen of the ship we learn, that from the moment when Captain Stark found it necessary to take this New York pilot aboard, Mr. Freeborn was indefatigable in his endeavors to save the ship and lives, but he split a new main-topsail and fore topsail in trying to keep her off shore, and all the head sails being crippled, was compelled to attempt to run her ashore.[62]

Freeborn's body was eventually recovered by the *Blossom*, the very boat from which he had boarded the *Minturn*.

The Blossom went down again on Saturday, and returned yesterday, bringing up eight bodies, including those of Thomas Freeborn, the Pilot, M. Thomas, Mr Ward and C.F. Hernell.[63]

After the dead were returned to their families, eulogized and interred, the press began to speculate on how these victims could have been spared:

Had the unfortunate passengers kept aft they would have saved their lives, as the cabin was, in all the gale, habitable, and would have been a complete protection. Three of the crew, Samson King, Daniel Mullen and J. Silvey, arrived yesterday, and made an affidavit of the facts of the wreck, before S. Baldwin, Esq, secretary of the Board of Underwriters.[64]

But speculation soon turned to blame, and the press went in search of scapegoats. The first criticisms were levied upon the wreck-master and the citizens on shore.

Had they done enough?

Were they cowardly?

The first of these salvos came from the men who were initially saved in the *Minturn's* longboat:

It is the opinion of the seamen saved, that no lives would have been lost, if proper exertions had been used on the shore. When Mr. Foreman was wreck master, he drew a surfboat several miles, at a gallop with horses, and saved the lives on the Austrian brig Astros, when the thermometer was 9 degrees below zero. On this occasion, the excuse was that there was no surfboat near. But it is proof that the crew off the New Jersey were saved at the same time by a good boat's crew.[65]

Next came the pointed accusations directed against Captain Stark for his aversion to New York pilots:

Freeborn died a martyr to his sense of duty and humanity – he will probably be found lashed, with his charge, to some part of the ship – and perished from his devotion to a good cause. But poor fellow – if Captain Stark had taken [Freeborn] on board in the morning as a friend, perhaps the ship and all would now have been in New York Harbor.[66]

Next the critics questioned the *John Minturn*'s upkeep:

In reference to the ship John Minturn, we are constrained by a sense of duty to say that the testimony warrants us in believing that she was not in a condition to navigate the coast at this inclement season. Seven of her survivors concur in the testimony that her sails were defective and that there were no spare sails on board. The witnesses are all mariners, some of them of much experience, one of them, Hugh Morrison, has been twelve years in the whaling service, and may be considered competent to judge of such matters. Most of her running rigging also is said to have been defective.[67]

However, contrary information was later gathered about the ship's condition, and the character of the sailors who survived was called into question:

We published on Tuesday a paragraph, from the report of the committee of the Shipwreck Society, to the effect that the committee were constrained "by a sense of duty" to say that the John Minturn *was not in a condition to approach the coast at this inclement season; that her sails were defective, and that she had no spare sails on board. We suppose, of course, that the committee had sought all available means of information, but we learn from a editorial in the Journal of Commerce this morning that they sought no information from the owners, nor do they seem to have had the testimony even of the only surviving officer of the ship. The fact is that the ship was furnished with new sails during the year 1845, and had spare sails and rigging in plenty. The committee, it seems, contented themselves with the testimony of the surviving seamen, in respect to which the Journal says:*

Sailors are very little to be trusted in respect to such statements. Those men were, under the circumstances, especially unworthy of credit. A part of them went ashore in the boat, and when near enough to jump on shore, let go of the rope, and so broke the connection with the ship, and left all on board to perish. During the long day in which their comrades on board were perishing, they refused all effort to reach her with the boat, though she was so near the shore that an attempt was made to throw a line to the mate, who had gone out on the bowsprit.[68]

Ten days after the demise of the *John Minturn*, a commercial vessel cleared New York Harbor, destined for New Orleans. She sailed under fair skies and hoped to complete the voyage in three weeks or less. Usually she sailed in tandem with the *Minturn*, but today Captain Sears of the ship *Orleans* sailed alone, mournfully passing the New Jersey shoreline in silent tribute to his fellow commander.

Unprincipled Wretches

For several years before 1846, persistent rumors circulated of the thievery and plunder of shipwreck victims by the Jersey shore inhabitants. The perception was that the latter sought out the wrecks for cash, jewelry and cargo, rather than provide assistance for those in need.

The rumors were hard to dismiss, reinforced when the wood from abandoned ships was frequently found in residents' homes, as weatherworn mantles and hard-backed chairs.

Shortly after the *John Minturn* disaster, ill sentiment toward the inhabitants found its way into a regional newspaper, *The New York Herald.* The timing was not a coincidence:

For many years prior to 1835, the Barnegat District of beach, on the coast of New Jersey, was renowned for the piratical propensities of the inhabitants, from Squire Platt the wreck master, and his boon companions, the parson and doctor of the interior town, down to the fishermen who lived on the beach, through all seasons, watching for, and sometimes ensnaring, their prey. Many a stout vessel has left her bones upon the beach. The Squire, the traders, tavern-keepers, and farmers, were waxing fat on their ill-gotten goods. From the ships General Putnam and George Canning, *wrecked in 1839, upwards of $40,000 worth of goods were stolen; and, although the goods were often seen with the thieves, the underwriters made no arrests. The undertaking was deemed too hazardous – all feared to begin. One schooner, with a hold full of goods and pine wood on deck, went on a trading voyage to the interior of North Carolina, and over $15,000 was realized. The thieves were emboldened by the apathy of the government and the Board of Underwriters, and their success was un-interrupted until 1835. Many tales are told of the diabolical means used to decoy vessels to their ruins. Fearful tales are related of horrid murders of passengers and mariners, but none of these charges have been proved. The dead tell no tales. There were so many awful accounts of this coast, extant, some of which were of course exaggerated, that the name of Barnegat was heard by the stoutest seaman with a shudder-the place, and all belonging to it, were to be avoided as a pestilence.*

In August 1835, Captain John Earl, and Mr. Jas. Bergen, were appointed agents for some fifty insurance companies, and took active measures to break up the horde of "moon cursers", as they were not inaptly called, on account of their hated to the honest face of that planet.

Every month will make these men worse. Where now is the energy that will break them up for another ten years-making them fear the jaws of the State prison? If the underwriters will not punish and banish the thieves, they should, with the assistance of the U.S. Government, maintain, for eight months every year, a guard upon the coast, with surfboats and men, and supply houses for wrecked seamen and passengers, short distances apart...Lives would be saved-piracies would be prevented-and smuggling would decrease...

The New York pilots have desired us to express their gratitude to Mr. Samuel W Thompson, for saving the body of Captain Thomas Freeborn, and in preventing his body from being robbed.

We deem it proper to state that the wreck masters and men, north of Squan Beach, are honest, fearless, skillful, and humane-affording good example of what "wreckers" should be at all times. We wish they could civilize their neighbors.[69]

The plundering of the *John Minturn* was first reported the very evening of the 15th, when the ship went to pieces:

As night came on, the wreck master offered ten dollars for every life which could be saved, but the useless boat he presented debarred all hope. He had but little command of his men, for, although he set guards on the ship, she was boarded that night and every passenger's trunk and seamen's chest, was cut or broken open and pillaged. The captain's chronometer was stolen, with about $1,000 in gold, which he had put in it, and locked and strapped securely. The box was found with the strap cut, and the chronometer and gold were missing.

A carpenter, who had three hundred dollars in gold, stayed on board, to try and save his sick brother. [The brother] was drowned and the dead body was robbed; for only $115 are reported as having been found upon him by the wreck-master.

Pork, lard and wrecked goods are being stolen at all points– and yet they imprudently charge the men saved seventy five cents for a bite of victuals and steal their clothing for pay.[70]

As reports of the *Minturn* disaster widened, many newspapers advanced the pirating theme further:

The *Newark Daily Advertiser:*

The Jersey Pirates-Accounts from the beach, where the John Minturn, and other vessels went to shore, in the late storm represent the conduct of the set of unprincipled wretches who infest that portion of the Jersey shore, as disgraceful in the extreme. Every body that has been recognized was found to be completely plundered of every article of value, the pockets turned inside out, and watches, rings, money, and other valuables unscrupulously appropriated by these detestable vampyres (sic).[71]

Reports followed of locals robbing bodies as they washed ashore and, in some instances, withheld the body until a fee was paid. These "wreckers" were a "brutal tribe of the surf" who danced gleefully as ships broke apart and lives were lost. Most often these accounts were found under the headline "New Jersey Pirates".

The *New York Herald*:

Humanity in New Jersey

It appears that those who lost friends in the late gale, on the coast of New Jersey, were compelled to pay ten dollars for each body cast lifeless on Swan Beach, to the local authorities in that vicinity. It is really to be hoped that none of those who thus exhort money, will ever be wrecked on their own shores. It would be difficult to tell what would become of their clothes and money, to say nothing of their souls.[72]

The savagery reported in New Jersey spread beyond the state's borders, reaching north and west:

From the *New Hampshire Sentinel*:

Twenty-two bodies have been recovered from the John Minturn wreck at New York on Friday. The captain, wife, son and daughter all lay together in the Methodist Church around the body of Mr. Keeler, a passenger was found a belt in which he is believed to have had $1000 and, if so, the corpse was robbed. In fact, every body found had been plundered by the Pirates of the Jersey shore.[73]

The *Boston Daily Bee* reported, almost word for word, an account from the *New Jersey Advertiser.*

The Cadiz Sentinel (Ohio):

New Jersey Pirates – The wretches who infest the shores of New Jersey, have been reaping a rich harvest of plunder by the late gale. Every body that has been discovered has been plundered by these wretches – the pockets had been turned inside out, And money, jewelry, and indeed every thing of value was stolen.[74]

In the *Democratic Pioneer* (Ohio):

Civilization and Barbarism.

The late accounts from the New Jersey coast where the John Minturn *and other vessels were wrecked in the gale of the 14th ultimo, represent that every corpse has been found plundered of every article of value, the pockets turned inside out, and watches, rings, money, and other valuable unscrupulously appropriated, by these worst then pirates–these hyenas preying on the dead. A thrilling rebuke to this conduct is given by a correspondent of the*

New York Gazette, which exemplifies the difference between civilization and barbarism.[75]

The New York Shipwreck Society was also anxious to learn about the facts and ran the following front-page advertisement.

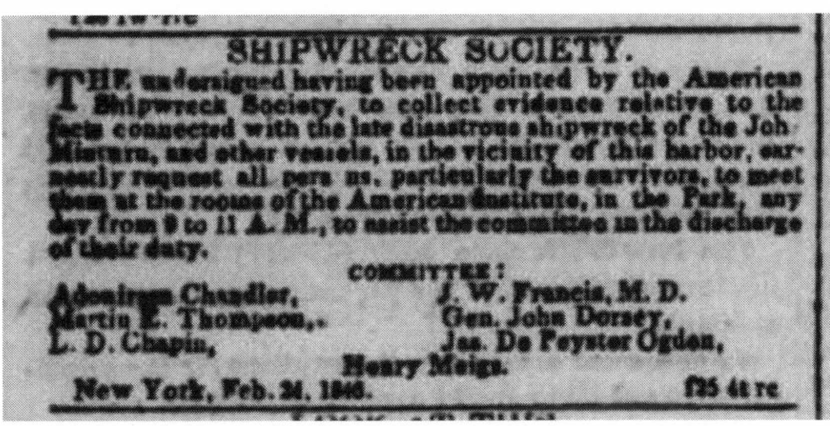

SHIPWRECK SOCIETY.

THE undersigned having been appointed by the American Shipwreck Society, to collect evidence relative to the facts connected with the late disastrous shipwreck of the Joh Minturn, and other vessels, in the vicinity of this harbor, earnestly request all pers ns, particularly the survivors, to meet them at the rooms of the American Institute, in the Park, any day from 9 to 11 A. M., to assist the committee in the discharge of their duty.

COMMITTEE:

Adoniram Chandler, J. W. Francis, M. D.
Martin E. Thompson, Gen. John Dorsey,
L. D. Chapin, Jas. De Peyster Ogden,
Henry Meigs.

New York, Feb. 24, 1846. f25 4t rc

Transcription:

The undersigned having been appointed by the American Shipwreck Society, to collect evidence relative to the facts connected with the late disastrous shipwreck of the John Minturn, and other vessels, in the vicinity of this harbor, earnestly request all persons, particularly the survivors, to meet them at the rooms of the American Institute, in the Park, any day from nine to 11 AM, to assist the committee and the discharge of their duty.

The would-be rescuers also received criticism:

For although there was broad daylight, no entreaty could induce the Jersey men to try to board [the Minturn*], although two of the seamen immediately offered to return with the surfmen. At ten o'clock there were many big-boned Jersey men on the beach...*[76]

It is the opinion of the seamen saved, that no lives would have been lost, if proper exertions had been used on the shore. When Mr. Forman was wreck master, he drew a surf boat several miles, at a gallop with horses, and saved the lives on the brig Astros, when the thermometer was 9 degrees below zero. On this occasion the excuse was that there was no surfboat near...[77]

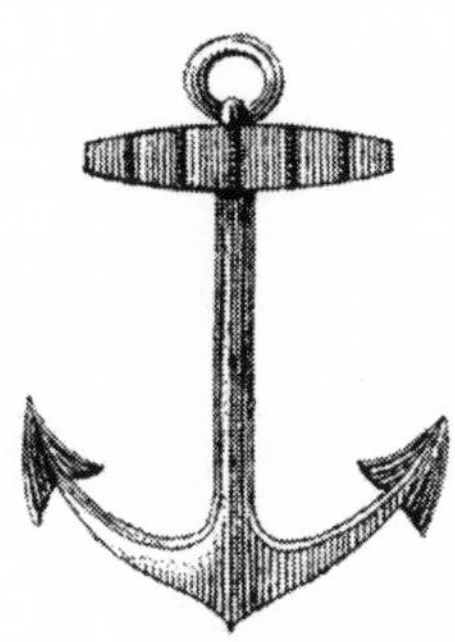

Elected officials from New Jersey viewed these damaging reports – and particularly the characterization of its shore-dwellers as "pirates" – as a huge blemish upon the state's reputation. The question was, who could legitimately rebuke the reports?

Editorials or investigations by New Jersey newspapers were ruled out. They would be discredited as biased and partisan. That left one alternative; a state sponsored "commission".

Investigation

In less than a month after the disaster, the New Jersey State Legislative established a commission to investigate the events that occurred on-shore during and immediately after the "*Minturn* Storm". They had a number of questions to consider:

- Were the pleas of shipwreck victims ignored?
- Were their possessions stolen?
- Was cargo looted?
- Were relatives of the dead charged a body "retrieval fee"?
- Did the inhabitants of the community refuse to aid in rescue and recovery?

The New Jersey official who proposed the investigation was a state senator by the name of Alexander Wurts.

We are rejoiced to see by our legislative reports that Mr. Wurts, the able Senator from Hunterdon, has called the attention of the Legislature to the recent outrageous conduct of the Barnegat Pirates on our coast.[78]

Wurts represented a New Jersey county far inland. His motivation for starting the investigation is unclear. Perhaps he had a political axe to grind against the representatives of the counties along the coast. Or perhaps he was assigned the task because he could provide an objective review.

The purpose of the investigation was clearly laid out in the public record. The state wanted to formally acknowledge every brutal newspaper claim against its citizenry and then have each charge separately addressed on a case-by-case basis. Only then could the matter be put to rest. They would review the claims by district, starting at the most northerly district first.

The following Preamble and Resolutions were introduced by [Senator Wurts] yesterday morning. We trust they will be adopted without a moment's unnecessary delay:

Whereas, it is represented in the public journals, that at the time of the late depressing shipwrecks of the John Minturn and other vessels on the New Jersey Coast, some persons on the shore neglected and refused to render relief and assistance to the perishing passengers and seamen, plundered the bodies of the dead of everything valuable found upon them, and in other cases exacted money for the delivery of the bodies; and whereas such charges require investigation, that if true, the inhuman and guilty actors may be punished to the utmost extent of the law, and proper and efficient means devised to prevent the repetition of conduct so barbarous and shocking: and if not true, that the state may be relieved from the odium of such barbarity.

One. Resolved, That the Legislature of New Jersey view with detestation and abhorrence, the conduct charged upon a portion of the people of the shore, at the time of said shipwrecks.

Two. Resolved, That the governor is hereby requested to ascertain the facts connected with the said shipwrecks, in relation to said charges, and communicate them to the legislature, with the recommendation of such further legislation, if any, as in his judgment may be necessary.[79]

Three commissioners were assigned to the investigation: P. Vredenburgh, Jr., John S. Darcy and John C. Ten Eyck. Of the three, Ten Eyck would later play a prominent role in state politics representing New Jersey as a U.S. senator during the Civil War.

The examination involved the testimony of thirty-six witnesses, as well as seven members of the New York Shipwreck Society. The approach of the committee was direct. They would investigate each shipwreck separately, assess the facts relative to the charges, and draw a conclusion about the actions of those on shore. Once all the shipwrecks had been assessed, the committee could then draw larger

conclusions of how the state's citizens responded to the disasters, and verify or refute the veracity of the newspaper claims.
Using a north to south reference for each shipwreck, they addressed them in order. Below is a summary of the findings.

The first review was of the pilot boat, *Mary Ellen*. It would also be the shortest:

The vessel which came ashore nearest Sandy Hook, on the morning of the 15th ult. was the New York pilot boat Mary Ellen, which was drawn high up on the beach. The crew all got safe ashore before any of the inhabitants could reach her... and that we have not heard of a charge against any person of illegally taking any thing belonging to the said vessel or crew.

With regard to the *Pioneer* , the schooner found off Fishtown, the committee found that resident Elias West performed heroically:

> ...[*West*] *provided every succor which kindness could suggest and was immediately tendered them, and that without inquiry whether they could pay or not. Had it not been for West, before other assistance could have reached them, they would probably all have been lost.*

The committee also found that under the watchful eye of resident Henry Wardell, "not one dollar of the wreck was suspected to have been illegally taken."

Next they reviewed the circumstances of the *Register,* the schooner found ashore opposite Long Branch. Recall that one of her sailors swam ashore and received assistance from residents Jacob Morris and Charles Bennett. It was due to their help that all of the *Register's* crew were saved.

> [*Those rescued*] *were so disabled by cold and exposure as to be unable to render any assistance to each other.* [*At Morris's home*] *every possible kindness and attention was furnished them with clothing, having been nearly stripped by the waves, and after remaining with him two days, were sent, by him, free of charge, to the Ocean House, where they embarked for New York.*

According to the commission, the body of the only fatality showed "not the slightest evidence or ground of suspicion that his body was robbed after it came ashore."
It was also found that the *Register's* cargo lay for two weeks untouched, scattered along the beach, "and up the ponds, undisturbed and without a guard".

The commissioners then concluded:

We are of the opinion that but for the assistance of Jacob W. Morris and Charles Bennett, two persons on the shore and citizens of this state, all the crew except the one who gave the alarm, would probably have shared the fate of the unfortunate passenger.

The three-man committee summarized their findings of the three wrecks in the northern district:

The above are all the wrecks in District 1 of which Henry Wardell is now the wreck master and there was no evidence as regards the wrecks of the Mary Ellen, the Pioneer and the Register, that some persons on the shore neglected and refused to render relief in assistance, plundered the bodies of the dead of everything valuable found upon them, and in other cases exacted money for the delivery of the bodies, nor is there any evidence that we could find, that one dollars worth of the property of these wrecks has been illegally taken.[80]

What the committee glossed over was that only one person was lost among the three wrecks, the unnamed passenger from the *Register.* Therefore the reference to the lack of evidence of the plundering of "bodies" or exacting of money for the delivery of bodies was an exaggeration.

The committee next turned their attention to the details of the four shipwrecks located in the second district, the area that extended from Long Branch to the "Squan", or Manasquan as it known today.

The first vessel reviewed was the schooner, *Arkansas.* Recall, she was beached near Deal with a crew of seven.

She was discovered by Charles McGinty ... and Cornelius Lane, both persons on the shore and citizens of the state. When they got there they found the vessel head on shore and the crew in the rigging, except one boy, John Woodward, who had already perished in the cabin, and the sea making a continual breach over her, the tide rising and the surf getting worse. The crew then, one by one, under the direction of Mr. McGinty and Mr. Lane, went out on the jib-boom, and jumping off into the surf, were caught by them before they were swept off by the sea, and carried safely to ashore. They all were nearly perished, and it was with difficulty that two of them were restored. The captain and the crew were immediately furnished with every comfort. We further report that the captain and crew were in imminent peril, one of their number had already perished, and their fate was probably but a few moments distant when they were rescued.

The details of the *Antares* wreck were reviewed next:

She came ashore about twenty miles south of Sandy Hook, just above Goose Pond...head on shore. The first and only person who discovered and came to her rescue, was William Conroe; he found the crew in the rigging and the sea making a continual breach over her. One of the crew came out on the jib-boom and threw a line which Mr. Conroe succeeded in catching; the person on the jib-boom then fastened a line around him and going down by another in the surf, was safely drawn by Mr. Conroe to the shore. This was repeated seven different times, until every one of the crew was brought to safety.

The last two wrecks examined in the second district were the barques, *New Jersey* and *Lotty*, which were found lying within a few hundred yards of one another. The *New Jersey's* commander, Captain Lewis, provided the strongest testimony countering the piracy and barbarity accusations.

The gentlemanly captain of the New Jersey, Edward Lewis, has voluntarily appeared before us and been examined under oath. We have ascertained from him that the only person on the shore when the New Jersey struck was Mr. Garret Newman, a citizen of this state, who immediately cried out to the crew not to attempt to come ashore without a line. She laid broadside to the shore. Mr. Newman, watching the retreating surf for half an hour, failed on repeated efforts to catch a rope thrown from the vessel, but finally, at the risk of his own life, succeeded. By means of this rope all got safely to shore in about fifteen minutes; they were immediately taken by Mr. Newman to his house and received every kindness and assistance he could give them.

The committee then entered into the legislature record the captain's praise of the local community:

Captain Lewis has also addressed a card of thanks to those who stood by him in his hour of peril, which he has given us permission to use, and from which we take the following extract:

To the people of Squan, north of Squan Harbor:

I, the master of the barque New Jersey, had the misfortune of being wrecked on your coast in the gale of the 15 February. We came on shore about half past six, a.m., the surf raging in such violence that it was almost impossible to walk or look to windward–but I leave that to be decided by those who were on the beach; and give my thanks and good wishes to the people as far as my acquaintance extends, for their honesty and perseverance. Also, for the immediate assistance which was rendered to us by Mr. Garrett Newman. To him we are indebted for our lives, as by his assistance we were enabled to secure a rope on shore, by which we were safely landed on the beach. Also, for a kind invitation to his small but hospitable roof, where we were received by the ladies and every assistance their means afforded, rendered to our number.[81]

The circumstances of the *Lotty* were then discussed. Because the wreck occurred within sight of many witnesses, extensive details were provided in the report:

By between nine and ten, a.m., the wreck master, John Remsen, and some thirty persons had collected at the wreck of the New Jersey, to save such property as might float ashore, when another vessel was seen a short distance to windward, struggling with the storm. All saw there was no hope for her. She soon struck between the outer bar and shore, and broaching to, swung her head seaward. The persons on shore and those on board spoke different languages. The wreck-master dispatched several men after the surfboat, while he attempted to get a line to the ship. The gallant Captain D'Haen, a strong and brave man, an expert swimmer, and who, it is said, had once saved his life in that way, deliberately fastened the ship's documents around him...The persons on shore followed him on the beach as fast as they could to render him assistance...

D'Haen eventually drowned and the men tracking him returned to assist in the rescues of the *Lotty's* remaining crew:

They then returned to the Lotty, the sea had knocked in the bulkhead of the house on deck, and swept, with its contents, the mate overboard. The wreck-master first made signs to those on board, to attempt to throw a line ashore, but they failed in that, two lines, one from the ship and one from the shore, were thrown at the same time, in hopes they would meet, but they did not catch; they then attempted to float a line ashore by means of a buoy, but it floated south instead of landward. Finally, one of the persons on the shore, accustomed to throw a squid when fishing in the surf, watching his opportunity, ran down in the receding surf and succeeded in throwing a fish line, loaded with lead, so far that its hook caught in some attached rigging floating to the leeward quarter of the ship. The fate of the Lotty hung upon that feeble line; by means of it a larger one was fastened to the ship. In the mean time, the persons sent for the surf boat, found that the violence of the gale was such that they could not keep it on the wagon, nor drive their horses against the storm.

Some thirty or forty then dragged it through the edge of the surf, over a mile, to the wreck of the Lotty. The surfboat having at length arrived, and a communication made with the ship by a rope, and another rope being fastened to the stern of the surfboat, the next thing to be found was "some persons on the shore" to man it. They were quickly found...and we report it to your Excellency as our opinion, from the evidence that those who ventured in the surfboat, were, at the time, exposed to greater peril than were those upon the ship. By the aid of the lines they approached the vessel-the crew descended into it-the stern rope parted, all were given up for lost, but the surf-men clung to the remaining rope, and by their aid the whole surviving crew of the Lotty was brought in safety to shore.

Captain Lewis from the *New Jersey* shared his perspective about the *Lotty*:

...there were at this time a number of men on the beach, they were sent for the surfboat, by John Remsen, the wreck-master, and returned in time to save them, although the surf was raging to such a height that it appeared impossible to take them off; but there were some true-hearted and daring men who risked their own lives to save those of the Lotty, and they succeeded in their first attempt. They were all taken to the house of Garret Newman, where their wet clothes were changed and they made comfortable. This happened under my notice while yet on the beach, I also state that the people

had no disposition to plunder, but used every means to save property and life, and gave the wreck-master whatever was thrown on the beach.

The committee summed up as follows:

We further report to your Excellency that not a dollar is suspected by the agent of the owners or the wreck-master to have been illegally taken, either from these wrecks or from the bodies of the dead; and that the charge that money was extracted for the bodies of the dead is expressed negatively.

The above comprises all the vessels wrecked in District No. 2 of which John Remsen, Esq., is wreck-master; and we report to your Excellency that there is no evidence or suspicion that any of the property of these wrecks has been illegally taken.

Moving south to district three, the committee turned to the circumstances surrounding the loss of the schooner, *Alabama*:

About eight miles south of the Lotty and New Jersey, and immediately south of Squan inlet, lay the scattered fragments of the wreck of the schooner Alabama, from Philadelphia to Boston, with hides, spices, iron & c. She came ashore on the farm of Thomas Cook, about half a mile from his house, and was first discovered by him about seven, a.m. on the morning of the 15th, broadside to the shore. He ran immediately down and found her rolling in the undertow, with two men in the rigging... Mr. Cook then ran home for a rope but before he could get back one of the (men) had been washed from his hold and the vessel gone to pieces. As the masts fell over towards the shore, the people caught the other from the rigging, *dead; and we report that from the time she was first discovered every thing that could have been was done to save the crew. What time she struck in that dreadful storm no soul has lived to tell. No doubt long through the night and morning their wild shrieks for help mingled with the tempest, but they were not in time...and every soul on board the Alabama perished.*

We report your Excellency that as regards the Alabama, there is no evidence we have been able to collect, that some persons on the shore refused and neglected to render relief and assistance to the perishing passengers and crew."

Once the committee had completed its review of the minor wrecks, they turned to the most serious disaster, that of the *John Minturn*. In particular their attention was drawn to the lack of assistance and timely aid.

The first persons who saw her from the shore, were George Johnson, James Dorset and John Van Note, as they stood near John S. Foreman's, about three and a half miles north of where she struck...The vessel struck upon the outer bar, about two hundred yards from the shore, where she lay until she went to pieces. Others, gradually through the day, as the news spread and they could make their way through the glades, came to the wreck. They first tried every means to throw a line aboard, as in the case of the Lotty, but in every attempt it fell short. They then attempted to float empty barrels with lines, but the surf immediately dashed them back upon them. Thus those on shore, as they came up, standing as far as they could in the surf, made use of every means in their power to establish communication with the ship. Every effort was found unavailing. The wreck-master, Hugh Johnson, got word of the wreck about one o'clock. p.m. He lived at the head of the bay, and his surfboat (the nearest one to the wreck), lay on the beach, about a mile from his house. He had been all the morning at the wreck of the Alabama, completely drenched by the rain and the surf. He immediately went to the Minturn, first sending word to his crew to bring the surfboat; but the wreck of the Alabama and other accidents had scattered the crew, and when he arrived at the wreck the surfboat had not come. He immediately dispatched one of his sons after it, but owing to the confusion of the moment, the nature of the beach, the distance the boat was off, and other difficulties fully detailed in his testimony, the boat could not be got to the wreck before sundown.

Testimony was now taken in the recovery of the *Minturn's* longboat onto the shore:

...The [Minturn] crew parted [the line] and the boat was carried by the current to the south. The people on shore followed it, and familiar from daily practice with the precise point of danger, as the boat neared the land, instantly formed a rope of hands, and with one of their ends resting on the shore, the others pushed into the sea, into the very power of the undertow, and as the waves were curling over it, at its moment of extremist peril, seized the boat and brought it to shore-another moment, and it would have been too late; she would have been drawn beneath the waters, and every one on board probably been lost. The boat was immediately bailed out by the persons on the shore, and drawn abreast the ship, the thoale-pins [§] fixed and additional oars procured. The wreck-master then offered $10, then $20, then any money to each man to venture off. They refused the money and said "We will go off without money as soon as with". During these offers the [Minturn's] crew of the long boat

---

§

A wooden pin or one of a pair, set upright in the gunwales of a rowing boat to serve as a fulcrum in rowing *were nearby, and were able to go off, if they saw fit, as the people on the shore; but the overwhelming weight of the evidence is that at no time, from the time the ship came ashore till she went to pieces, could the surfboat, if she had been there, been put off through the surf and lived. The dangers of the surf were also greatly increased by the floating spars around the vessel, rendering it almost certain, in the opinion of the most experienced, that even if a boat could have got through the surf, it would have been broken to pieces by the floating spars.*

Night and darkness drew near and yet no means of communications with the ship occurred. The sailors who had come ashore in the long boat were taken about sundown by William Aiken to his own house, where they made their home till they left the beach, and for which he has never asked of them or received any pay. But the "persons on the shore" were not driven off by the cold or wet or hunger. All day long had they been on the beach exposed to the rain, standing in the surf and drenched with water; but they remained there to render all possible assistance to the perishing passengers and crew.

The final minutes of the *John Minturn* were now recalled in great detail:

About ten o'clock at night a piercing cry came from the vessel to the shore; she had yielded to the power of the storm and gone to pieces...Most of the passengers and crew were swallowed up in the waters...In the darkness of the night, from the tumultuous waters, they called for help, and [many] responded to the call. The sea was so full of wreck stuff, dashing violently in the surf, that it endangered their lives. They first attempted to push the long boat out, and succeeded twice in getting the boat so near that they drew two men ashore. In order to get the boat out it was necessary to go to windward with a line fast to her to keep her from going beyond the reach and capsizing; they thus stood in the surf up to their middles, and the waves breaking over their heads, pushing her out, and all held from being carried away in the surf by the line from the shore; but the boat was so unmanageable and so dangerous to handle, one of their number getting disabled, that they drew her out.

They learned of one initial survivor who died shortly afterwards:

Joseph Borden then ran down into the surf as far as he could, and threw a line on the forward part of this fragment of the wreck, so that it was caught by one of the "perishing crew". Mr. Borden then told him to make it fast around his waist...and he was drawn to the shore alive. He was then carried to the shanty.

They then at first thought that all alive on that part of the wreck were ashore, when they heard a groan. Then Mr. Borden and Peter Sutphin succeeded in getting to this piece of the wreck by means of a rope. They went to where the man was groaning, and Mr. Borden said to him, "My dear fellow help yourself all you can, and we will do all we can to help you". He was sitting bent over, leaning his head on his knees, unable to help himself, or to speak, and by his side nine of his companions dead. They took him and helped him carefully over the wreck. By this time Taber Sherman had got on and assisted them. They got him to the edge of the wreck, and then, with the assistance of others was taken to the shore and carried to the shanty, where he died in about half an hour.

More details of rescues were then reviewed and conclusions reached regarding the *Minturn*:

The above facts are ascertained from the most unquestionable testimony; and we are of the opinion, but for this assistance rendered, that long before the morning light, all would have perished, and the last moan of human suffering ceased upon the wreck. Nor did the exertions of the men cease with these efforts. Several of them remained on that beach, their wet clothes frozen on them, without change, with no protection from the cold but getting behind the casks, night and day, until Tuesday evening, guarding the property and the bodies of the dead.

We, therefore report to your Excellency, that there is no proof, as regards the John Minturn, that "some persons on the coast neglected and refused to render assistance to the perishing passengers and seamen". On the contrary, we report that, in our opinion, the records of the surf can show few more persevering, enduring and courageous efforts to save the perishing passengers and seamen than were shown by Monmouth surfmen on this occasion; and that, but for such efforts, the fate the Alabama would have been re-enacted, and very soul on board the John Minturn perished.

We further report to your Excellency, that we have given but one day's history of these hardy surfmen. From the earliest settlement of the state, ever since commerce first began to send her sail along the coast, they have ever stood ready to render every relief and assistance to perishing passengers and crews. Within that time many a ship's crew and passengers have been by them taken through the surf, the accounts of which, if we should report them to your Excellency, would fill volumes.

The next charge is that these persons on the shore plundered the dead bodies of every thing valuable found upon them. The evidence is that the violence of the current carried many of the bodies from ten to twelve miles south of the wreck, and that within that distance, forty-five dead bodies came ashore; that immediately a guard was set and persons employed to watch and draw them from the surf, and that as it was done some covering was placed over their persons, that as they were found, up to Friday, they were taken to the coroner; that some of the persons, with outward signs of wealth and large amounts, in fact, about them, lay for five or six hours, if not longer, on the beach, with persons passing to and fro until late in the evening, and yet all their effects were faithful delivered to the coroner.

The committee next addressed the supposed fee for the retrieval of bodies:

As regards the charge that money was exacted for the delivery of the bodies, we report that the coroner, on his own responsibility, employed persons to watch the dead as they were drawn from the surf, till he could send for them; that he hired teams to go along the beach for sixteen miles after them, as they were found...and to watch them day and night until the friends could come for them; that he prepared coffins and buried those for whom no friends came; and upon an estimation, it was thought that such expenses would reasonably amount to $12 or $13 each; and that the coroner deemed it right and proper that when friends came for the bodies, those of them that had money and could afford it, should pay such expenses only as he had thus become responsible for. But the payment of such expenses were never made a condition precedent to *the delivery of the body. It was never asked of a friend if he could pay or not.*

We, therefore, report that there is no evidence that money was exacted for the delivery of the bodies, and believe the charge to be utterly untrue.

The commission's only finding of fault was minor, the theft of some items in a sailor's trunk:

There have been other charges in the public journals against persons on the shore, which, perhaps, it may be expected that we should report upon. It has been charged that there was wholesale plundering from the wrecks of the Minturn and Alabama-bands of people standing on the shore and seizing every thing by violence as they came up. Such charges we believe to be utterly untrue.

We report to your Excellency one act of peculiar atrocity. On the afternoon or evening of the 15th February, the trunk of Captain Babcock ...floated ashore, and was taken charge of by an agent of the wreck-master, and placed with three others in a heap, and a guard set over them. When the wreck with the survivors neared the shore, all hands were called to assist in getting those on board from the wreck, the guard at the trunks among the rest. While the guard was so engaged, some person or persons, citizens of this state, went off with the trunk of Captain Babcock, and cutting the straps and breaking open the lock, pillaged it of its contents.

And we report to your Excellency, that a guard was stationed at the cabin part of the wreck, where the captain, officers and cabin passengers would naturally have their trunks; and that, by the direction of the wreck-master, no person was permitted to go until Monday afternoon, except those belonging to the ship; and that while the wreck-master had gone down the beach on his official duties, some of the sailors and steerage passengers of the Minturn, were seen repeatedly to go into the cabin and overhaul the contents of the chests and trucks which still remained there, to carry away packages, articles of clothing & c. And that, in our opinion, if any thing was illegally taken from the cabin, it was not done by any citizens of the state.

The commission then closed the report by dismissing all the accusations made in various newspapers. Not only did they refute all the rumors, they went so far as lavishing praise on the men and the women of the shore:

The commissioners appointed in pursuance of the resolution adopted by the legislature of the 5th instant, relative to the shipwreck of the John Minturn and other vessels on the New Jersey coast, having investigated the charges in the resolution referred to, and it being shown by the report and accompanying proofs, that the said charges are not only not sustained, but that the conduct of the citizens resident near the shore, on those lamentable occasions, was distinguished by intrepidity and humanity-Therefore,

Resolved. That the Legislature (the House concurring) of the State of New Jersey, have read and considered the report and proof aforesaid, with hearty satisfaction; and that the conduct of the citizens and authorities resident at, and having charge of the coast, as detailed in said document, is deemed high meritorious, honorable to themselves and the state.

Today it is difficult to assess if the specific and overall findings were accurate or not. Some have charged the investigation was a whitewash [82] by New Jersey officials.

The report was soon made public, which added a greater sense of weight to its findings. Through the *Minturn* tragedy the state finally had its opportunity to publicly remove the stigma that had tarnished its citizens for decades.

Epilogue

The bodies of those who could be identified were returned to their loved ones. Some were never identified, either because of their battered and bloated condition or some families were unaware that their loved ones had been aboard, particularly in the case of the *Cherokee* sailors who hastily boarded the *Minturn* after their own disaster.

Even today, little information is known about many of the victims. Many bear no first names, where they resided or if they were passenger or crew:

- Theophylact Bache, a passenger, whose funeral was held on February 26 at St Paul's Church, New York
- Christian F. Hernell, aged 20
- Lewis Jones, Western New York
- Samuel Vincent, Plattsburgh, New York
- John Coster (painter), Mass.
- Martin Marsden, Brooklyn
- J.L. Ward (butcher), New York
- Theodore Beach, New York
- (Two) Unknown Irishmen

- Unknown Englishman, wife and two children
- Mr. Blancher, Maine (about 28)
- Hugh Morrison, Milwaukee, Wisconsin Territory
- John Kohler and wife, Chambers Street, New York City
- Mrs. Forbes
- Mr. Forbes (servant)
- John Leeds, Mystic, Conn.
- Mrs. Baker
- Mr. Palmer, Stonington, Conn.

And there were a number of smaller tragedies within the larger disaster. For instance, there was a newlywed couple, the husband returning to New York to surprise his mother with his bride:

Mr. Kohler was a native of New York, where he has a mother and sisters. He left the city several months ago, and a particular friend received a letter from him a week or two before that he was coming home in the John Minturn; that he had been married to a young lady, and intended to bring his wife home and not to tell his mother or any of his folks, as he meant to surprise them. They both perished in the wreck, and the surprise was a truly heart-rendering one, particularly to his aged mother, of whom he was the only son. He and his young bride were yesterday laid side by side in the same grave, affording a sad reflection as the fallacy of human calculations and hopes. [83]

Others who perished referenced the *John Minturn* on their tombstones. Captain Joseph Babcock and Nicholas Baker, the two crewmen from the *Van Buren,* intended to return home to family and friends in Rhode Island:

Extraordinary Mortality- A correspondent in Wickford, R.I., informs us that a very unusual number of deaths has recently occurred among the prominent inhabitants of that village. Two men, viz. Capt. Joseph Babcock, and Nicholas F. Baker, were lost with the ill-fated ship John Minturn. They had been wrecked on a bar near Corpus Christie, and had taken passage on board the [John Minturn], for their families and friends, after an absence of about seven months, who from letters before, expected soon to meet them again in the family and social setting. The affliction from its suddenness was exceedingly bitter. Both were married men, the former left two children, the latter his aged parents dependent upon him for support... [84]

Captain Babcock was interred in Elm Grove Cemetery in North Kingston, not far from where, as a boy, he caught his first views of the bay and the great ocean beyond:

His inscription reads:

In Memory of Capt. Joseph B. Babcock Who Perished on the Wreck of the Ship John Minturn near Squam (sic) Beach. 16 Feb 1846 in his 35th *Year*

First mate Nicholas Baker is buried nearby:

His inscription reads:

In Memory of Nicholas F. youngest son of Benjamin and Ruth Baker who perished in the Wreck of the Ship John Minturn, near Squan Beach, N. J., February 15, 1846, Aged 25 years, 10 months, 1 day

There were also two brothers aboard, both employed as carpenters who were buried side by side. Nelson Harding (age 25) and Hiram (age 22) are buried in a common coffin in Vosburg Cemetery, Wyoming County, Pennsylvania.

Their father, George, and brother in-law, James Bunell, made the winter's journey to New Jersey to claim the bodies and bring them home to be buried by the river among the hills they had loved as children. [85]

But the most information published about the *Minturn* victims was reserved for the Stark family and Thomas Freeborn:

The melancholy loss of the ship John Minturn has thrown our little community [Mystic Bridge, Ct] into mourning, for the loss of nearly a whole family. Captain Dudley Starks (sic) had three children, two of whom, with his wife, were on board the ill-fated ship. His oldest daughter [she was not aboard the ship] is the wife of David Mallory, merchant, of this place. No one can conceive the grief and distress of Mrs. Mallory on hearing of the loss of father, mother, brother, and sister...Captain Starks' children. Lost in the above ship, were named Stephen D, aged 15, and Helen, aged 12 years. Mrs. Catherine Starks [Dudley Stark's wife] was the daughter of Simeon Hailey, Esq, of Mystic. [86]

Captain Stark, his wife Catherine, son Stephen and daughter Helen were interned side by side in a graveyard in Stonington, Connecticut:

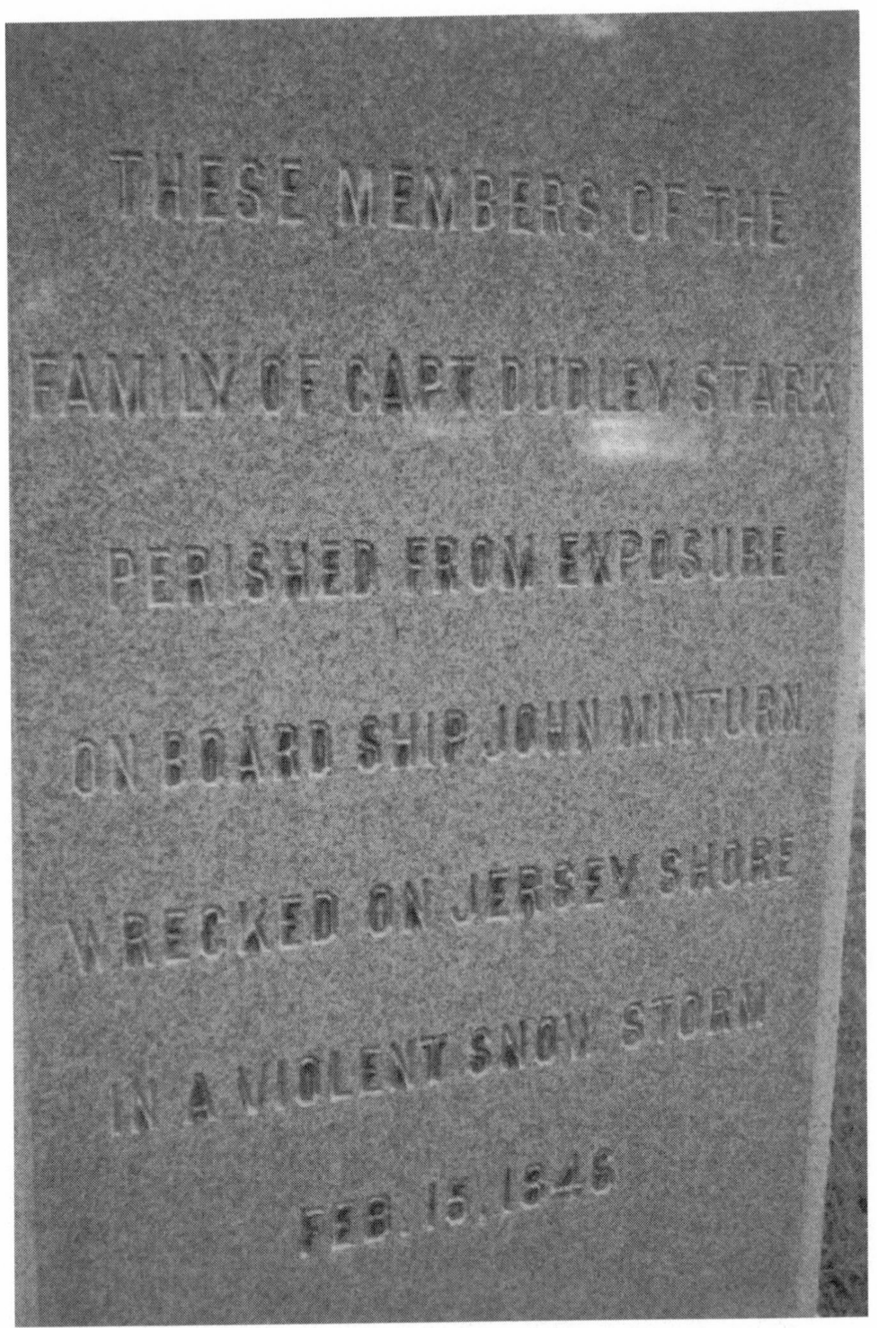
THESE MEMBERS OF THE
FAMILY OF CAPT DUDLEY STARK
PERISHED FROM EXPOSURE
ON BOARD SHIP JOHN MINTURN
WRECKED ON JERSEY SHORE
IN A VIOLENT SNOW STORM
FEB. 15. 1846

Transcription:

THESE MEMBERS OF THE FAMILY OF CAPT DUDLEY STARK PERISHED FROM EXPOSURE ON BOARD SHIP JOHN MINTURN WRECKED ON JERSEY SHORE IN A VIOLENT SNOW STORM FEB. 15, 1846

HIS WIFE
DUDLEY & C. H. STARK
STEPHEN D.
AGED 15 YEARS
HELEN A.

It was after the burial that more information about Dudley Stark became known, not all of it flattering. His estate was probated in early April, less than two months after his death. The administrator was his son-in-law, David Mallory, and the following posting appeared in the local newspaper:

THE Court of Probate for the District of Stonington has appointed the first Tuesday of April, 1846, at 10 o'clock, A. M., at the Probate Office in Stonington, in said district, for the appointment of Commissioners to receive, examine and allow the claims of the creditors to the estate of Capt. DUDLEY STARK, late of Stonington, deceased, represented insolvent, when and where, before said Court, all persons interested in said estate are notified to appear, if they see cause, and be heard relative to said appointment.

DAVID D. MALLORY, Adm'r.

Stonington, march 10 91 [87]

Transcription:

The Court of Probate for the District of Stonington has appointed the first Tuesday of April, 1846, at 10 o' clock, A.M. , at the Probate Office in Stonington, in said district, for the appointment of Commissioners to receive, examine and allow the claims of the creditors to the estate of Capt. Dudley Stark, late of Stonington, deceased, represented insolvent, when and where, before said Court, all persons interested in said estate are notified to appear, if they can cause, and be heard relative to said appointment.

David D. Mallory, Adm' r

A meticulous inventory of Stark's assets was then complied, listing every item, some valued less than one dollar. The assets ranged from a Mahogany Table ($12.00), to Portraits ($5.00) to "Broom and Brushes" (50 cents).

A list of Dudley Stark's assets

On the other side of the ledger, the debts and the large number of creditors were listed, including one of the *Minturn's* victims and fellow resident of Stonington, a "Mr. Palmer".

Names of Creditors	Amount presented	Nature of Claim	Date	Interest		Amount allowed
Amount brought forward $						2521.68
Cottrell & Howe	126.14	Note	Feb 26 '58	15.11	141.25	
" "	17.62	Book acc		2.64	20.26	189.51
Joseph Cottrell	14.00	Note	Feb 26 '58	1.37		15.37
[illegible] Howe	8.82	Book acc		25		9.17
Williams & [illegible]	15.88	Book acc		31		16.19
Charles G. Beebe	1.08	Book acc				1.08
Isaac D. [illegible]	29.03	Book acc		1.25		42.28
Lyman Dudley	17.73	Book acc		2.12		19.85
[illegible]	13.62	Book acc		80		14.42
David Mallory	3.26	Book acc		20		3.46
[illegible] Palmer	89.07	Note	Feb 25 '58	8.72	97.79	
" "	2.50	Book acc			2.50	100.29
Mystic Bridge Co	1.00	Book acc				1.00
[illegible]	2.57	Book acc				2.57
[illegible]	9.00	Book acc		22		9.22
Isaac C. Holmes	2.89	Book acc		10		2.99
[illegible] Randall	1.00	Book acc				1.00
[illegible]	1.67	Book acc				1.67
[illegible]	30.00	Book acc				30.00
[illegible]	2.86	Book acc				2.86
George [illegible]	10.75	Book acc				10.75
Nathaniel [illegible]	6.00	Book acc				6.00
Charles P. Williams	24.07	Book acc				24.07
Joseph [illegible]	14.09	Book acc				14.09
[illegible]	3.00	Book acc				3.00
Cyrus [illegible]	10.26	Book acc		1.80		12.06
						2055.76

A list of Dudley Stark's creditors

Report of
Commissioners on
Estate of Capt
Dudley Stark

Report of Commissioners on Estate of Captain Dudley Stark

Amount allowed	Names of Creditors and amount		Folio	Date	Interest	Amt allowed
2521.68			Amount brought forward			2055.79
	Henry & Brown	16.59	Book acc			16.59
159.57	M. C. Church	5.50	Book acc			5.50
15.37	Peter Bouryet	94	Book acc			94
9.67	James Mitchell	2.10	Book acc			2.10
16.19	Jeremiah Holmes	25.12	Book acc		4.14	29.56
1.08	Daniel C. Edgcomb	7.01	Book acc		84	7.85
42.25	Wm Meeker	2.92	Book acc			2.92
19.55	Champlin & Allen	57.78	Book acc		4.62	62.40
14.42	S. McIntire	48	Book acc			48
3.46	Elisha Rockham	3.01	Book acc			3.01
[illegible]	Edwin A. Gallup	5.72	Book acc			5.72
100.29	C. C. Bouryet	5.50	Book acc			5.50
1.00	[illegible]					
2.57						
9.22						
2.99						
1.00						
1.67						
30.00						
1.86						
10.75						
6.00						
24.57						
14.69						
3.00						
14.06						
3055.76						

New London County
Probate District of Stonington May 1. 1846

On this sd day personally came Jesse Gallup and Amos C. Fish esquires, and took the oath prescribed by Law for Commissioners on Insolvent Estates, as commissioners on the Estate of Capt Dudley Stark late of Stonington deceased represented Insolvent.

Before me Asa Fish Judge of Probate for the District of Stonington

Dudley Stark's Estate documents (continued)

To the Court of Probate for the District of Stonington –

We the subscribers, having been appointed by said Court, Commissioners to receive, examine and allow the claims of the several Creditors to the Estate of Capt. Dudley Stark late of Stonington dec'd, represented insolvent, having been duly sworn to a faithful and impartial discharge of the duties of our appointment, and having given notice to the Creditors of the deceased agreeably to the direction of our commission by advertising in the Peoples Advocate published in New London April 15th 1826, and by posting the same on the public sign post same day nearest the place where the dec'd last dwelt. Have attended to the service assigned us, and present to said Court a true list of all the claims that have been presented to us, with the sums we have allowed on each.

Interest allowed to Oct 15th 1826

Names of Creditors	Amt. presented	Nature of Claims	Date	Interest	Amt. allowed	
Asa Fish	$1090.98	Note	Sept 10 1824	$137.69	$1228.67	
" "	75.00	Endorsement	" 15 1825	4.91	79.91	$1152.66
" "	267.21	Book acct		8.01		275.22
						$1427.88
Ashby Pool & Co	109.97	Note	Feb 27 1825	10.72		120.69
Simeon Haley	600.00	Note	Sept 1825	21.20		621.20
John Brown	311.00	Note	Aug 7 1824	40.89		351.89
				carried forward		$3521.61

Dudley Stark's estate documents (continued)

The accounting confirmed the estate was insolvent; his debts far outweighed his assets. This meant there was nothing he could pass on to the surviving daughter, Mrs. Mallory[**] and Dudley Stark's creditors would not be repaid in full.

For all of Stark's hard work at sea, his investments and risks during his fifty-one years, he lost everything, including the lives of most of his family. His financial losses were now laid bare for the entire community to see.

While the death of Captain Stark and his family may have shaken a small Connecticut community, the death of Thomas Freeborn reverberated throughout New York City, deeply affecting the men from the New York Pilots Association:

At a meeting of the New York Pilots Association, held on the morning of the 24th of February, James Mitchell was called to the Chair, and Edward Hope was appointed Secretary-The Chairman announced the death of Captain Thomas Freeborn, who perished at his duty, as pilot of the ship John Minturn, at Squan Beach, New Jersey, on Sunday, the 15th Instant; and the mournful, but consoling,

---

[**] Perhaps the wife of the administrator of the Stark's estate

intelligence that his body had been recovered, and was to be buried at 3 P.M. from the house of his afflicted mother. After many members had given a feeble expression to their feelings, the following preamble and resolutions were passed unanimously:

Whereas, it has pleased Divine Providence to take among us-whilst enjoying the full vigor of manhood and health-our associate, THOMAS FREEBORN, who has been endeared to us by every tie that can bind manly hearts together-and whilst recognizing in him the finest specimen of that strict integrity in business relations, and that lofty honor in social intercourse, which ever marks the valuable citizen, the good son, and the kind brother, we have the melancholy pleasure of knowing that he lost his life in the high performance of his duty as a New York pilot-a lot that may befall us all-but for which we can only hope, that God, in his mercy, will permit us to be well prepared as our beloved associate, who has gone before.

Resolved. That the members of this Association will attend the funeral, at the proper time and place.

Resolved. That we will wear the usual badge of mourning, for thirty days, as a mark of respect to our deceased brother.[88]

The funeral was a notable, even by New York customs in 1846. The New York newspapers provided great details:

FUNERAL OF MR. FREEBORN, THE NEW YORK PILOT.—It having been announced that the funeral of Mr. Freeborn, who was drowned in the late gale, would take place at three o'clock yesterday, long before that hour his friends began to assemble, to pay the last tribute to the deceased. The solemn and sad rites being performed, the procession was arranged in the following order:—

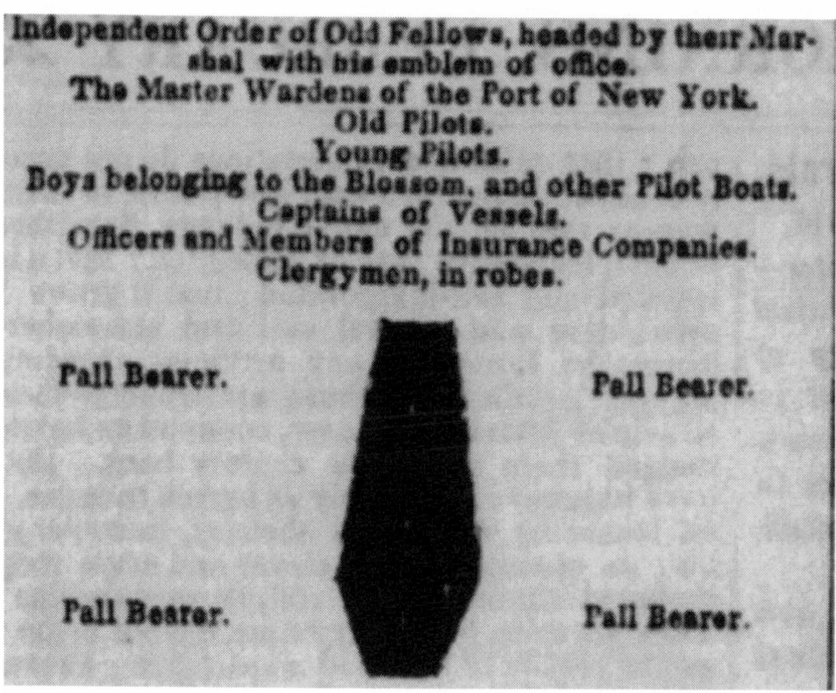

Independent Order of Odd Fellows, headed by their Marshal with his emblem of office.
The Master Wardens of the Port of New York.
Old Pilots.
Young Pilots.
Boys belonging to the Blossom, and other Pilot Boats.
Captains of Vessels.
Officers and Members of Insurance Companies.
Clergymen, in robes.

Pall Bearer. Pall Bearer.

Pall Bearer. Pall Bearer.

Citizens,
To the number of two thousand, two and two.

The procession moved at half-past three o'clock, and proceeded, on a slow walk, up Orchard to Grand street, thence to the Bowery, along the Bowery to Stanton, down Stanton to Forsyth, and up Forsyth to the burial ground. On reaching the entrance to the burial ground, the Society of Odd Fellows formed an avenue, through which the corse was conveyed, and on going through the gate, the minister commenced reading the solemn service for the dead—"I am the resurrection, and the life," &c. The coffin was deposited near the vault, and the minister continued the service; after which the corse was lowered to its place The brother-pilots and near relatives of the deceased gathered round the vault, and during the service, we observed many of the hardy survivors in tears. Those brave fellows who have battled with a thousand storms, and braved danger in every form, could not resist the impulse of nature, and had to give vent to the overflowing of their hearts. It was a melancholy satisfaction to the surviving friends of the deceased to see the very large concourse of mourners that attended him to his resting place, and it shows that he carried to the grave with him that respect which was manifested towards him when living. Thus the lamented Freeborn, after being rocked and toss-ed on the ocean during life, at last rests at ease in his narrow home.

The tributes to Freeborn continued well after the burial. In fact, his "burial" in the vault was only temporary. The Pilot's Association went to great expense to build a huge structure in Brooklyn's Greenwood cemetery and moved his remains from the Rutgers Street Burial Ground. There, a large marble monument "consisting of a carved sarcophagus on a stacked base, topped with an obelisk" [89] was erected.

Monument erected to Thomas Freeborn

Base of monument

Standing as it does, upon one of the highest points of the Cemetery, this monument is a very conspicuous object, and for a very considerable distance is in full view of vessels, as they move up and down the bay.

The monument may be considered as resulting from a combination of ideas, most of which are naval. From a massive face, rises a square sarcophagus. Upon this rests the ship's capstan, but the cable, which is coiled about it is severed. The pillar, which rests from the capstan, maybe regarded as a mutilated mast. On the summit stands Hope, still retaining her anchor, and pointing heavenward… on the front of the sarcophagus a sea storm and shipwreck are represented in relief." [90]

This tempest wants blue soft and fair-
This storm gust bright, pictured air,
These torrents rushing from the sky,
Were dews below, or clouds on high.

The fires, in boreal flames that played
So softly o'er last evening shade
Now fierce altwart the darkness glare
Driving, with fork bolts, the air.
These angry waves, that swell and roar
Late broke in ripples on the shore,
Or where yon sea dogs rend their prey,
Calm as a sleeping infant lay.

Swift and secure the sea-boy glides
But ah! What peril near him hides;
Beneath him, or above him cast
The sunken rock, or furious blast.

Christian! Thy pilot walks the wave
Full wise to guide-full strong to save:
His faintest word shall still the roar
Of winds, and bear the safe to shore.

Freeborn's monument stands much as it did in 1846. It is only one of two icons that remind us of that horrific Sunday, and what happened aboard the *John Minturn*. And although Thomas Freeborn lost his life that day, he will forever live as one of "Natures Noblemen".

He was one of "Natures Noblemen", whom admirable qualities invest in the dignity in every walk of life; and whose career is always radiant as the bright track of a shooting star. Long may his towering monument allure the eye of his survivors to aspire, like him, to greatness; and repose at last upon the elevation to which all men look up with general homage. [91]

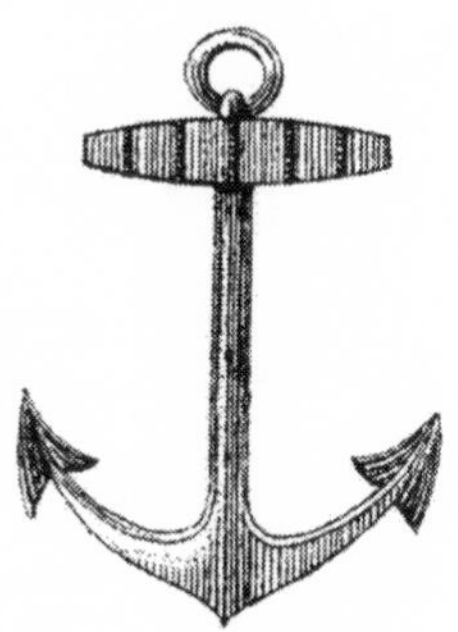

Shadowed and lost behind some non-descript bushes and a sprawling tree sits the most understated of the two memorials to the *John Minturn*. It is located in Point Pleasant and pedestrians likely take it for a decorative lawn ornament.

The tribute is easily overlooked. Hardly anyone takes the time to read the commemorative plaque.

The dedication reads:

In Memoriam

To The Victims of the

Packet Minturn

Lost At Sea In A Storm Off

Our Coast

Feb. 15. 1846

The bottom of the anchor appears to be sinking into the ground. In the fall and winter, leaves and snow almost entirely cover it.

However, I sincerely hope this retelling of the events will finally rescue the *John Minturn* from the obscurity of the past.

May those lost rest in peace.

Hurl'd on the beach, behold, they gasp! They bleed!

And groaning, cling upon the' illusive weed;

Another billow bursts in boundless roar!

Arian sinks! And Memory views no more!

Ah, total night and horror here preside!

My stunned rear tingles to the whizzing tide!

It is the funeral knell! And gliding near,

Methinks the phantoms of the dead appear.

But lo! Emerging from the watery grave,

Again they float incumbent on the wave!

Again the dismal prospect opens round,

The wreck, the shore, the dying and the drown'd

And see! Their hold no longer they retain,

They sink, overwhelm'd, and never rise again.

Author's Note

If, after reading this account of the *John Minturn* storm, you wish to contribute more information about the event, there are two ways to do so.

One is through my blog, which provides additional information about the *Minturn,* and can be found at *ThomasGClark.net.* On the right hand side, towards the bottom, you will see a listing for the *John Minturn.* I will share the latest updates there.

Or you can email me directly at ThomasClark1234@Gmail.com (it will also appear as "History Revisited" in any reply).

Lastly, if you believe there is a shipwreck or event that is worthy of another book akin to *Undiminished Violence*, please let me know. I'm always anxious to fill in overlooked history.

All the Best! Tom Clark

Bibliography

- *America's Victory: The Heroic Story of a Team of Ordinary Americans And How They Won the Greatest Yacht Race Ever,* by David W. Shaw, Sheridan House, 2004
- *Inland Passage: On Boats & Boating in the Northeast*, by David W. Shaw, Rutgers University Press, 1998
- *The Youth's History of the United States*, by Edward Sylvester Ellis, volume 4, 1887
- *Tales of Shipwrecks and Adventures at Sea: Being a Collection of Faithful Narratives of Shipwrecks, Mutinies, Fires, Famines and Disasters, Incidents to a Sea Life, Together with Celebrated Voyages, Amusing Tales Tough Yarns and Interesting Anecdotes*, by James Lindridge, William Mark Clark, 1846 - Seafaring life
- *Hazard's United States Commercial and Statistical Register,* Volume 5, edited by Samuel Hazard, 1841

- *Journal of the Proceedings of the Senate of the State of New Jersey*, 1846
- *The Oxford Companion to Ships and the Sea*, Oxford University Press, Peter Kemp, 1976
- *Great Storms of the Jersey Shore,* by Larry Salvadore and Margaret Thoas Buchholz, Down the Shore Press, 1993

Acknowledgements

I would like to thank the following individuals and organizations for their help in completing this book:

- Jamin Wells via https://shipsontheshore.wordpress.com
- Pat Schaefer, Collections Access and Research Mystic Seaport: The Museum of America and the Sea
- Sal Marino, Point Pleasant Beach Historical Society

Article I. Index

T

U

V

W

---

1. The-Crankshaft Publishing web site: http://what-when-how.com/new-jersey/shipwrecks-to-shrewsbury-borough-new-jersey/
2. The-Crankshaft Publishing web site: http://what-when-how.com/new-jersey/shipwrecks-to-shrewsbury-borough-new-jersey/
3. Boston Post, January 16, 1846
4. TexMaps website- 3/10/17 http://www.texmaps.com/corpus-christi-bay-1845.html

5. *Boston Morning Post*, Boston, Massachusetts, Friday, January 12, 1838
6. *Boston Post*, Boston, Massachusetts, Saturday, December 13, 1845
7. Wikipedia Commons, retrieved 3/10/17, General View of the Naval Academy, Annapolis, Maryland, a wood engraving after a drawing by W. R. Miller (Miller, William Rickarby, 1818-1893), published March 1853 in Illustrated News, New York, New York.
8. Wikipedia Commons, retrieved 3/10/17 H. S. Knapp - A History of the Pioneer and Modern Times of Ashland County. Philadelphia: J. B. Lippincott & Co. (1862)
9. *Boston Post*, Boston, Massachusetts, Thursday, April 17, 1845
10. Credit: Pittsburgh Prints from the Collection of Wesley Pickard, c.1843-1982,AIS.2006.03 Archives Service Center, University of Pittsburgh
11. Wikipedia Commons, retrieved 3/10/17 , John Roebling
12. "The Bridges of Pittsburgh" ,Wikipedia Commons, retrieved 3/10/17
13. *Boston Post,* Boston, Mass. January 27, 1846
14. *Boston Post,* Boston, Massachusetts, Wednesday, August 13, 1845
15. *The Columbian Magazine* , November 1848, "The Pilot"
16. *Tales of Shipwrecks and Adventures at Sea: Being a Collection of Faithful Narratives of Shipwrecks, Mutinies, Fires, Famines and Disasters, Incidents to a Sea Life, Together with Celebrated Voyages, Amusing Tales Tough Yarns and Interesting Anecdotes*, by

James Lindridge, William Mark Clark, 1846 - Seafaring life - 948 pages
17. *An Abstract of the Laws of the State, and Ordinances of the Corporation of the City of New York in Relation to Vessels, Wharves, Slips, Piers, Basins, Wrecks & Salvage*, Herald Book and Job Printing Company, 1845
18. Wikipedia Commons , retrieved 3/10/17
Map of the Colony of Rhode Island , https://upload.wikimedia.org/wikipedia/commons/d/d1/A_map_of_the_colony_of_Rhode_Island,_with_the_adjacent_parts_of_Connecticut,_Massachusetts_Bay,_%26c._(4579312892).jpg
19. According to one source, the John Minturn was painted "bottle green" with a white stripe. And curiously, it had thirteen simulated "gun ports" on either side. [1]

[1 Asbury Park Press, Asbury Park, New Jersey, February 15, 1981
20. Per Jamin Wells via https://shipsontheshore.wordpress.com
21. *Hazard's United States Commercial and Statistical Register*, Volume 5 edited by Samuel Hazard see: https://books.google.com/books?id=yoo3AQAAMAAJ&pg=PA301&dq=snow+gale+october+1841&hl=en&sa=X&ved=0CEMQ6AEwBmoVChMI5KuH_oWiyAIVSSoeCh2gAQxg#v=onepage&q=snow%20gale%20october%201841&f=false
22. Ibid
23. Ibid
24. *The New York Herald,* February 22, 1846
25. *The New York Herald*, February 17, 1846
26. *The New York Herald,* February 18, 1846
27. *The New York Herald,* February 17, 1846
28. *The New York Herald*, February 19, 1846
29. *Boston Post*, Boston, Massachusetts, Monday, February 16, 1846,
30. *The Farmer's Cabinet,* Amherst, New Hampshire, February 19, 1846
31. *The Farmer's Cabinet,* Amherst, New Hampshire, February 19, 1846
32. *The New York Herald*, February 22, 1846

33. *Morning News*, New London, Connecticut February 16, 1846 , Page 2
34. *Gettysburg Star and Republican Banner*, Gettysburg, Pennsylvania, February 20, 1846
35. *Boston Post* , Boston, MA. February 17, 1846 Note the ship is most likely the *Democrat*
36. *Boston Post* , Boston, MA, February 18, 1846
37. *Boston Post,* Boston, MA, February 17, 1846
38. Ibid
39. Ibid
40. *Boston Post,* Boston, MA Tuesday, February 17, 1846
41. *Boston Post*, Boston, MA, February 19, 1846
42. Ibid
43. *The New York Herald,* New York, February 18, 1846
44. *The New York Herald,* New York, February 17, 1846, "The Terrible Storm".
45. *Times-Picayune*, New Orleans, Louisiana, Sunday, January 25, 1846, Page: 3
46. *Boston Post*, Boston, Massachusetts Thursday, February 5, 1846
47. *America's Victory: The Heroic Story of a Team of Ordinary Americans And How They Won the Greatest Yacht Race Ever,* by David W. Shaw, Sheridan House, 2004

https://books.google.com/books?id=OQE5LLL2xx4C&pg=PR6&lpg=PR6&dq=America's+Victory:+The+Heroic+Story+of+a+Team+of+Ordinary+Americans+--+And+How+They+Won+the+Greatest+Yacht+Race+Ever&source=bl&ots=-r2tyWtVmm&sig=BfA9eNPNezMiCIWQPGRdgJn-M_4&hl=en&sa=X&ved=0ahUKEwjI6LmgvsDSAhVU3mMKHWqgBTEQ6AEIMTAE#v=onepage&q=America's%20Victory%3A%20The%20Heroic%20Story%20of%20a%20Team%20of%20Ordinary%20Americans%20--%20And%20How%20They%20Won%20the%20Greatest%20Yacht%20Race%20Ever&f=false

48. Ibid
49. Ibid
50. *The Youth's History of the United States*, by Edward Sylvester Ellis, volume 4, 1887

51. *Vevay Indiana Palladium*, Vevay, Indiana February 28, 1846
52. *The Charleston Mercury*, Charleston, S.C. Feb 23, 1846, page 2 "The Storm"
53. *The Alleganian,* Cumberland, Maryland, February 27, 1846
54. *Boston Post*, Boston, February 18, 1846, "By Last Night's Mails"
55. *Vevay Indiana Palladium,* Vevay, Indiana, February 28, 1846
56. *Indianapolis Indiana State Sentinel*, Indianapolis, Indiana, March 12, 1846
57. *London St. James Chronicle Whitehall and General Evening Post*, London, March 17, 1846
58. *Daily Sentinel and Gazette,* Milwaukee, Wisconsin, March 11, 1846
59. *The Alleganian,* Cumberland, Maryland, February 27, 1846
60. *Boston Post,* Boston, February 25, 1846
61. *New Hampshire Sentinel*, published as New-Hampshire Sentinel. (Keene, New Hampshire), March 4, 1846
62. *The Alleganian,* Cumberland, Maryland, February 27, 1846
63. *New Hampshire Sentinel*, published as New-Hampshire Sentinel, (Keene, New Hampshire), March 4, 1846
64. *Indianapolis Indiana State Sentinel*, Indianapolis Indiana, March 12, 1846
65. *Vevay Indiana Palladium,* Vevay, Indiana February 28, 1846
66. *The New York Herald*, New York, February 18, 1846
67. *The Sun*, Baltimore, March 6, 1846, page 1
68. *The Commercial Advertiser*, New York, March 5, 1846
69. *The New York Herald*, February 25, 1846, Coast Piracies-The Barnegat Pirates
70. *New Hampshire Sentinel,* Keene, New Hampshire, March 4, 1846
71. *Newark Daily Advertiser* (Newark, New Jersey), Saturday, February 21, 1846
72. *The New York Herald*, February 23, 1846, page 2
73. *New Hampshire Sentinel*, March 4, 1846
74. *The Cadiz Sentinel*, March 4, 1846
75. *Democratic Pioneer,* Upper Sandusky, Ohio, March 20, 1846
76. *The Alleganian,* Cumberland, Maryland February 27, 1846
77. Ibid

---

78. *Newark Daily Advertiser,* Newark, New Jersey, February 26, 1846
79. *Journal of the Proceedings of the Senate of the State of New Jersey*, 1846 , page 589 See Google Books:

https://books.google.com/books?id=JBwZAAAAYAAJ&pg=PA589&lpg=PA589&dq=john+minturn,+The+journal+of+the+proceedings+of+the+senate+of+new+Jersey&source=bl&ots=kyqP0bZX_z&sig=ttUdaOdDNXSpkNRO3i41karC6Yg&hl=en&sa=X&ved=0ahUKEwjAqpPMu8fSAhUD0mMKHRgEDBYQ6AEIJjAB#v=onepage&q=john%20minturn%2C%20The%20journal%20of%20the%20proceedings%20of%20the%20senate%20of%20new%20Jersey&f=false
80. Ibid
81. Ibid
82. *Inland Passage: On Boats & Boating in the Northeast,* by David W. Shaw
83. *American and Commercial Advertiser*, Baltimore, February 26, 1846, "Closing Scene of a sad Calamity"
84. *The Christian Watchman*, Boston, Mass, March 20, 1846, "Variety"
85. Find-A-Grave, Nelson Harding, retrieved 3/10/17 : https://findagrave.com/cgi-bin/fg.cgi?page=pv&GRid=86752470
86. *New York Herald*, February 23, 1846, "The Loss of the John Minturn"
87. *People's Advocate* , New London, Connecticut, Wednesday, March 25, 1846 Volume: VI Issue: 32 Page: 4
88. *The New York Herald*, February 25, 1846
89. *America' s Victory: The Heroic Story of a Team of Ordinary Americans*, by David W. Shaw, Sheridan House, 2004
[90] Greenwood, A Directory for Visitors, by N Cleveland, 1852 https://books.google.com/books?id=Hlo-AAAAYAAJ&dq=wreck+of+the+John+Minturn+A+R+Ward&source=gbs_navlinks_s
91. *America' s Victory: The Heroic Story of a Team of Ordinary Americans*, by David W. Shaw, Sheridan House, 2004

Made in the USA
Middletown, DE
07 February 2021